Menander: *Epitrepontes*

BLOOMSBURY ANCIENT COMEDY COMPANIONS

Series editors: C. W. Marshall & Niall W. Slater

The Bloomsbury Ancient Comedy Companions present accessible introductions to the surviving comedies from Greece and Rome. Each volume provides an overview of the play's themes and situates it in its historical and literary contexts, recognizing that each play was intended in the first instance for performance. Volumes will be helpful for students and scholars, providing an overview of previous scholarship and offering new interpretations of ancient comedy.

Aristophanes: Frogs, C. W. Marshall
Aristophanes: Peace, Ian C. Storey
Menander: Samia, Matthew Wright
Plautus: Casina, David Christenson
Plautus: Curculio, T. H. M. Gellar-Goad
Terence: Andria, Sander M. Goldberg

Menander: *Epitrepontes*

(The Arbitration)

Alan H. Sommerstein

BLOOMSBURY ACADEMIC
LONDON • NEW YORK • OXFORD • NEW DELHI • SYDNEY

BLOOMSBURY ACADEMIC
Bloomsbury Publishing Plc
50 Bedford Square, London, WC1B 3DP, UK
1385 Broadway, New York, NY 10018, USA
29 Earlsfort Terrace, Dublin 2, Ireland

BLOOMSBURY, BLOOMSBURY ACADEMIC and the Diana logo are
trademarks of Bloomsbury Publishing Plc

First published in Great Britain 2021
This paperback edition published 2023

Cover design: Terry Woodley
Cover image: Wall Fresco, House of the Menander, Pompeii. Artist unknown.
The Print Collector / Alamy Stock Photo

A catalogue record for this book is available from the British Library.

A catalog record for this book is available from the Library of Congress.

ISBN: HB: 978-1-3500-2364-2
        PB: 978-1-3502-2668-5
        ePDF: 978-1-3500-2366-6
        eBook: 978-1-3500-2365-9

Series: Bloomsbury Ancient Comedy Companions

Typeset by RefineCatch Ltd, Bungay, Suffolk

To find out more about our authors and books visit www.bloomsbury.com
and sign up for our newsletters.

Contents

Figures

Preface

I am most grateful to Lily Mac Mahon and her colleagues at Bloomsbury Publishing for the help they have given me throughout the difficult gestation of this volume. My thanks are also due to Microsoft for having stored my draft text in 'the cloud', unknown to me, until I fortuitously discovered it in February 2020 when I had thought it would be necessary to abandon the project after a burglar or burglars stole my laptop and the USB stick that was plugged into it, to Ms Katerina Evangelatos for enabling me to choose an illustration from a set of photographs of her late father's production of *Epitrepontes*, to Dr Stavroula Kiritsi for putting me in touch with her and for making me aware of this epoch-bridging production in the first place, and to the series editors, Niall Slater and C. W. (Toph) Marshall, who read my final draft and made numerous valuable suggestions; but above all to William Furley, not only for his splendid, innovative edition of *Epitrepontes* but for reading and commenting on the whole of my final draft, supplying two illustrations, and making available to me his draft edition of, and commentary on, the passages of which our knowledge has been enriched by the new Michigan fragments. As always, responsibility for any surviving errors rests solely with me.

Alan H. Sommerstein
Nottingham, September 2020

Note on Transliterated Greek Words

When any Greek word is transliterated for the first time in the text or endnotes, the letters eta and omega are represented by ē and ō respectively (*ekklēsia, archōn*); at subsequent occurrences of the same word, plain *e* and *o* are used. This rule also applies to Menandrian play titles and character names (*Geōrgos*, Sōphronē), but not to other proper names which are generally given in their traditional 'latinized' form (Demetrius, Cephisia).

Menander the Athenian

Menander (Menandros), son of Diopeithes, an Athenian citizen of the deme (district) of Cephisia,[1] was born in the Athenian year corresponding to 342/1 BC[2] and died in his fifty-second year (291/0).[3] During his lifetime the Greek world underwent profound changes. At the time of his birth it comprised a thousand or so city-states (*poleis*) in the old Greek homeland, on the coasts and islands of the Aegean, and at many other places (mostly on or near the sea) in the Mediterranean and Black Sea basins, from Massalia (Marseilles) to Salamis on the east coast of Cyprus and from Cyrene (in modern Libya) to Borysthenes (at the mouth of the Dnieper in what is now Ukraine), in most of which Greek colonists had lived for two to four hundred years (in Cyprus for nearly a thousand); most of these remained fiercely independent of each other (though some were subject to foreign rulers – those on the mainland of Asia, for example, were part of the Persian empire) and most of them were what would now be called republics, either oligarchic (with all power in the hands of an aristocratic or wealthy minority) or, like Athens, democratic (with an assembly of all adult male citizens as the effective decision-making body). Athens was one of the largest of these *poleis*, and memories of the glorious days (478–405) when she had dominated two or three hundred tribute-paying 'allies' tempted Athenians to believe that their *polis* was, or ought to be, much more powerful than her resources actually allowed her to be.

By the time of Menander's death all this had been utterly transformed. Defeat by Philip II of Macedon in 338 had made Athens, in effect, his vassal. Then, after Philip's assassination in 336, his son Alexander III ('the Great') had invaded Asia and conquered the whole of the Persian empire, from Egypt to Tadjikistan and north-western India, only to die in 323, aged thirty-three, leaving no heir (his only son, born posthumously, was never more than a mascot and was quietly murdered at the age of about twelve). For some forty years thereafter Alexander's generals, or their heirs, fought over the division of his dominions, which eventually crystallized into three major and several minor kingdoms, and sought to make allies, or vassals, of the principal *poleis* of old Greece.

Several of these *poleis*, including Athens, had revolted against Macedonian domination immediately after Alexander's death, only to be defeated by his regent in the west, Antipater, who abolished Athens' democracy (imposing a property qualification for political rights), had its leading statesmen executed or exiled (the most famous of them, Demosthenes, avoided either fate by taking his own life), and established a regime of willing collaborators whose position was assured by the posting of a Macedonian garrison on the hill of Munychia, dominating the Peiraeus. After Antipater's death in 319, his successor Polyperchon allowed the democracy to be restored, and many of the collaborationist leaders were put to death, but scarcely a year later Antipater's son Cassander gained control of Athens and appointed Demetrius of Phalerum, an intellectual (once a pupil of Aristotle) of broad interests and considerable talent, as 'manager' (*epimelētēs*) of Athens with autocratic power.

Demetrius governed Athens for ten years until 307. Another of the competing dynasts, Antigonus the One-Eyed, wishing to enlist the *poleis* of Greece as his allies, had promised them autonomy in a decree issued back in 315, and he now sent his son, another Demetrius (afterwards known as Demetrius the Besieger (*Poliorkētēs*)), to liberate Athens. Demetrius destroyed the fortress at Munychia, full democracy was restored, and the Athenians decreed extraordinary honours to Demetrius and his father, designating them 'saviour gods' and appointing a priest for their worship.

When Antigonus and Demetrius were defeated (Antigonus being killed) by a coalition of other kings (most of the Macedonian dynasts had by now taken this title) at Ipsus in 301, Athens declared itself independent, but soon afterwards, during a serious famine, a general named Lachares seized power[4] (with the backing of Cassander) and ruled Athens until 295 when he was expelled by Demetrius. Demetrius re-established a garrison at Munychia and also at the Museum hill just outside the city itself. The democratic constitution was nominally retained (as it had been during the rule of Lachares), but Demetrius (now established as king of Macedonia) intervened increasingly to secure outcomes and leaders acceptable to himself. Thus during Menander's adult lifetime Athens had experienced at least six regime changes, but in one respect things had not changed at all – she had virtually always been effectively dependent on some Macedonian overlord, though sometimes able to play off one dynast against another.[5] It is striking that all regimes retained the basic institutions of the classical democracy, the assembly (*ekklēsia*) open to all qualified citizens and the council of five hundred (increased to six hundred in 307)[6] and all described themselves as democracies, even that of 322–318 which deprived over half the citizen body of the right to speak and vote in the assembly.[7]

Menander survived all these vicissitudes, though on one occasion he got into difficulties. He was friendly with Demetrius of Phalerum, and it is noteworthy that two of his eight first prizes at the major state festivals were won in the first two years of Demetrius' rule; when Demetrius fell, an attempt was made to put Menander on trial, but he was saved by the intervention of Telesphorus, a cousin of Demetrius Poliorcetes.[8] That Menander was regarded as a sympathizer by opponents of full-blown democracy is suggested by the erection of a statue to him, prominently placed in the theatre of Dionysus, apparently quite soon after his death and therefore under the regime of 295–287 which was looked back on as an oligarchy. However, the most strongly political passage of his work that survives, the report of a local assembly meeting at Eleusis in Act IV of *Sikyōnioi (The Sicyonians)*, has distinctly pro-democratic implications: the assembly takes a decision which is both humane and correct, there are frequent interjections from the floor which are all in support of the better cause, and a crusty oligarch who believes that tearful, emotional pleas are usually bogus (150–3) and that a small committee is more likely to get at the truth than a large assembly (154–5) is shown to be completely wrong.[9] Very possibly this play was written between 307 and 301, the only substantial period during Menander's career when a more or less unfettered democracy was in existence.

At the age of eighteen, like other boys of the better-off classes, Menander became one of the 'ephebes' (see Henderson 2020) who for two years lived a semi-segregated life of military training, garrison service, frontier patrols and various ritual activities; another member of this ephebic cohort was the future philosopher Epicurus. Before graduating into full adulthood, in the spring of 321, he had produced his first play, *Orgē (Anger)*,[10] the first time anyone had done so while still an ephebe.[11]

Menander's total output was stated by one ancient writer (Apollodorus of Athens, second century BC) to have been 105 plays; others put it at 108 or 109. This is far more than can have been staged at the major Athenian festivals, the Lenaea and City Dionysia, in a career of about thirty years (even if, improbably, Menander was selected as a competitor at every possible opportunity), and many of his plays must have had their first performance at local theatres in various parts of Attica (or even in other regions, if he either paid a visit or sent a script).[12] As mentioned above, he won only eight victories at the two major festivals, but probably none of his contemporaries did any better (see Konstantakos 2008); his most famous rival, Philemon, in a far longer career (he lived to be ninety-nine), was victorious at the Lenaea only three times. The early commissioning of a statue (see above), and the creation soon afterwards of a series of murals depicting scenes from his plays (see Chapter 9), suggest that by the time of his death he was regarded in influential circles as a dramatist of truly exceptional talent.

We have it on the authority of Plutarch (first/second century AD) that Menander improved with age. Speaking with special, but not necessarily exclusive, reference to Menander's adaptation of style to his characters' age and personality, Plutarch says that 'if one compares Menander's early works with his middle and later ones, one can judge how much further still he would have advanced had he lived longer'.

Unfortunately we cannot in general date enough of Menander's plays with enough accuracy to be able to follow any evolution in his style or technique. It does, admittedly, appear that satirical references to living individuals are found only in early plays (before about 314); but a play may have no such references and yet still be early, as is the case with *Dyskolos (The Curmudgeon)*, produced in 316. Those who have speculated about the date of *Epitrepontes* have generally thought it to be a late play, but until recently there was no real evidence on the question. William Furley (2009a: 249) suggested that the metaphorical use of *phrourarkhos* 'garrison commander' might indicate the presence of a Macedonian garrison in Athenian territory, and therefore a date in or before 307 or (more likely) in or after 294; then in 2011 Eric Handley, re-examining a papyrus fragment of an ancient headnote (Hypothesis) to the play (*Oxyrhynchus Papyrus* 4020), originally published in 1994, argued that one line of which only the first three letters, *epi*, survive, had given not an alternative title for the play (the usual title, *Epitrepontes*, appears in the next line) but its date, 'in the year of So-and-so', So-and-so being the *archōn* (chief magistrate) for the year in question. If so, the *archon*'s name cannot have had more than six letters – and it so happens that during Menander's adult life there was only one *archon* whose name was as short as that: Nicias, who held the office in 296/5. The proposals of Furley and Handley are of course incompatible, and neither of their arguments is conclusive; we must still say that we do not know the date of *Epitrepontes*.

Menander's plays were still being read and copied as late as the seventh century A D, but by the ninth they had disappeared completely, though a few readers of contemporary theological texts written on recycled parchment might perhaps have been able, had they tried, to discern traces of the half-effaced words of a comedy script. All that then remained of Menander were a collection of about a thousand one-line maxims (the so-called *Monosticha* or *Sententiae*),[13] only a minority of which were actually by the poet whose name they bore; several hundred scattered quotations of passages, lines or single words by other ancient authors; and some adaptations of his plays by the Roman dramatists

Plautus and (especially) Terence. These latter, however, existed only in the West, which conversely, until the fourteenth century, knew nothing of the Greek material preserved by the scholars and scribes of the Byzantine empire and in one or two monasteries beyond its borders. The modern rebirth of Menander began in 1844 at one of these monasteries, on Mount Sinai (see Chapters 3 and 9), and fragments of ancient manuscripts (usually all called 'papyri', though many of them are actually written on parchment) still continue to emerge from long burial in Egypt. Today we possess one play (*Dyskolos*) virtually complete, and enough of half a dozen more to have at least a fair idea of their overall structure; altogether there are about twenty identifiable plays from which enough papyrus material survives to make them worth including in an edition, and several more which would meet that criterion if only they could be identified. Altogether it is likely that not much less of Menander's scripts survives than of those of, say, Aeschylus.[14] *Epitrepontes* is one of the better-preserved plays, though as we shall see there are still some important questions about its content that we cannot answer with any assurance.

2

Menander and New Comedy[1]

Contests for choruses of *kōmōidoi* (literally 'revel-singers') were established at the Athenian festival of the (City) Dionysia in 486 BC, and during the next two or three centuries the dramatic genre thus first officially recognized spread, first to the outlying localities (demes) of Attica, then to the rest of the Greek world, and finally to the vastly expanded Greek-speaking world created by Alexander's conquests and, in modified forms, to some non-Greek-speaking peoples as well, notably the Romans. The stone inscriptions recording the contest results at the Athenian Dionysia and Lenaea were periodically updated until about 135 BC, but we know of Athenian comic dramatists active later than this, and there is no good reason to suppose that they were unable to produce their works in the venerable theatre of their native city. Records of competitions elsewhere are numerous in the second century AD, and some continue into the third, as at Thespiae (Boeotia) and Aphrodisias (Caria) (Roueché 1993; Manieri 2019a, b). This long history can be divided into two phases: two hundred years of rapid evolution, followed by half a millennium of virtual stasis.

Aristotle, who left Athens in 323 BC and died a year later – just too soon to have seen any of Menander's plays – has little to say about comedy in the *Poetics* as we have it, but some remarks in chapter 9 capture an important aspect of the development of the genre during the fourth century:

> It is evident from what has been said that the job of a poet is not to say *what happened*, but *what can happen* . . . by necessity or probability. . . . This makes poetry more philosophical and more serious than history; for poetry speaks rather of universals and history of particulars. By 'universals' is meant the question 'what sort of person will necessarily

or probably[2] say or do what sort of thing?', which poetry aims to answer, giving names to the characters; by 'particulars' is meant [for example] 'what did Alcibiades do, or what happened to him?' This has now become clear in the case of comedy: they construct a plot on the basis of probability and then give the characters random names, and do not write about particular individuals as the iambic poets[3] did.

Poetics 1451a36-b15

Most of the comic poets of the fifth century had written about 'particular individuals' too (consider Aristophanes' portrayals, or caricatures, of Socrates, Euripides or Cleon), and when Aristotle wrote the transition had not yet been completed. One dramatist, Timocles, was writing plays of Aristophanic inspiration and high political content, with numerous references to contemporary individuals,[4] and even Menander, as we have seen, included some such references in some of his early plays. But broadly speaking Aristotle's generalization holds true, and scholars of Hellenistic and Roman times followed his lead by dividing the history of comedy into three phases – Old Comedy (Aristophanes, his contemporaries and his predecessors), Middle Comedy (dramatists who made their debuts between *c.* 390 and *c.* 340) and New Comedy (Menander, his contemporaries and his successors), a classification that came to influence all study of the genre.[5] In reality there were of course no hard and fast boundaries between the phases, and the preferences of authors and of audiences alike changed incrementally rather than abruptly, but viewed over the whole period from, say, 405 (Aristophanes' *Frogs*) to 316 (*Dyskolos*) the transformation was so great that we would hardly believe, if we did not know it to be true, that New Comedy was a direct descendant of Old.

New Comedy appears to have been dominated (though not monopolized)[6] by plots in which the driving force was heterosexual love,[7] usually (though not invariably) viewed from the male perspective, and the goal of the action was either the achievement of a desired union (sometimes a marriage, sometimes a relationship with a *hetaira*)[8] against opposition from one or more quarters or (as happens in *Epitrepontes*, and also in *Misoumenos [The Man She Hated]* and *Perikeiromenē [Her*

Shaven Head]) the re-establishment of an existing union after it had been disrupted.

The formal structure of New Comedy is very simple. Every play, it seems, consisted of five acts, separated by choral interludes. The chorus was still, as it had always been, an essential part of the performance, but it had virtually no role in the drama. It was conventional for a character to remark, at the end of the first act, on the approach of (usually) a band of drunken youths (as at *Epitr.* 169–71), and then to make an exit so as to avoid getting in their way; but in the surviving Menandrian texts the chorus is never, after that point, mentioned at all, except that at each act-break there is a notation *khorou* ('<performance> of the chorus'). We cannot even tell by direct evidence whether the chorus only danced or whether they also sang (probably the latter, if only because bands of drunken youths are more usually noisy than silent), nor what they did during the acts,[9] nor whether they departed after their last interlude or remained to the end of the play (probably the latter, since they would then be able to sing appropriately in accompaniment to the festive final exit of the principals).

Within the acts, almost all the verse was spoken, though a few plays contained an occasional solo song.[10] The action was in principle continuous within each act, though sometimes the scene may be briefly empty of actors between an exit and the next entrance.[11] No more than three speaking characters are ever on stage at any one time,[12] and it is likely, though not certain, that the plays were always written so as to be performable by a troupe of three actors.[13]

The imaginary location of the action was normally a street or other public space outside two (sometimes possibly three) private houses;[14] each of these houses might belong to a head of family (like young Charisios in *Epitrepontes* or the elderly Nikēratos in *Samia [The Woman from Samos]*), to a bachelor (like young Chairestratos in *Epitrepontes*, elderly Smikrinēs in *Aspis [The Shield]*, or the soldiers in *Misoumenos* and *Perikeiromene*), or to a *hetaira* (as in *Dis Exapatōn [The Double Deception]* and *Synaristōsai [The Ladies' Lunch]*). Other persons or families of significance to the action might be imagined as living at a little distance (like Smikrines in *Epitrepontes*, Kallippidēs in *Dyskolos*, or the farmer Kleainetos in *Geōrgos [The Farmer]*) or may arrive during the play as visitors from further afield (like Dēmeas in *Misoumenos*). The action of the drama is essentially the *inter*action of these family members and individuals.

The characters are usually assignable to a limited number of stock types (Ruffell 2014), who appear to have been fairly readily recognizable, even before they spoke or were spoken to, by their masks and costumes. The main categories were: young citizen men (unmarried or newly married); older citizen men[15] (of an age to have marriageable children); marriageable maidens (or recently married wives), and young women of obscurer status who are eventually discovered to be marriageable; *hetairai*; professional soldiers; parasites (men who tried to live, so far as possible, at other people's expense); brothel-keepers, male or female (*pornoboskoi*); hired cooks; slaves or ex-slaves of both sexes and all ages. This is a very limited and skewed sample of society – but it is all that is needed to make a typical New Comedy plot work; and in Menander's hands it was capable of almost infinite variety, because, in the words of Louis MacNeice,[16] he knew 'all the tricks of the virtuosos who invert the usual': he delighted in creating characters who failed to behave in the manner expected of a person of their type and putting them to work in generating new plot structures.

New Comedy resembled tragedy, and differed markedly from what we know of Old Comedy, in that it was usually in broad terms predictable how a play would end. The young man in love would gain the bride he desired; the couple on the point of splitting up would come back together; the soldier reported dead would come back alive and well. Frequently, too, the audience, early in the play, would be let into secrets that remained unknown to the characters or most of them, by means of a prologue spoken by an omniscient divinity – sometimes at the outset of the play (as in *Dyskolos*), more often, it seems, as probably happened in *Epitrepontes*, after an opening scene or scenes had aroused their intrigued curiosity. With the conclusion therefore largely known in advance, most of the plot interest would therefore lie in uncertainty about how it would be reached and in the detours that might arise along the way. The divine prologue-speaker in *Epitrepontes* no doubt told us that Charisios and Pamphilē would be reunited, and that the baby exposed in the woods was safe and well and would soon be identified as the son of Pamphile and of Charisios too; but the route to this destination is long and devious, including a considerable period during which Charisios, and most of the other *dramatis personae*, believe the baby to be Habrotonon's and it seems more than possible that Charisios may take her as his new partner, and meanwhile Smikrines becomes more and more determined to ensure that far from being mended, his daughter's marriage shall be ended – until a seemingly flukish coincidence (Pamphile and Habrotonon both being out of doors at the same time) leads to the discovery of the truth. Or *was* it just a flukish coincidence? Habrotonon thinks that 'one of the gods' must have taken pity on Pamphile and Charisios (874). In *Dyskolos* the divine prologue-speaker, Pan, assures us (36–44) that he and the Nymphs who share his shrine will secure a highly desirable marriage for Knēmōn's daughter, and through the play we are encouraged to see their influence behind the series of events that lead to this dénouement. Did the divine prologue-speaker in *Epitrepontes* say something similar?

We have seen that no more than about half, if even so many, of Menander's plays received their first performance at one of the two major Athenian festivals, but *Epitrepontes* was in all probability among those that did. If the papyrus Hypothesis (see p. 5) did indeed state the date of the first performance, that would settle the matter, since these two dramatic festivals were probably the only ones, and certainly the only ones in Attica, whose records could be readily consulted by researchers; and in any case the fact that *Epitrepontes* was selected, not long after Menander's death, for inclusion in a series of paintings of scenes from his comedies (of which the Mytilene mosaics – see Chapter 3 – are a distant descendant) indicates that it was one of his best-known plays and hence was probably produced on a big occasion before an audience drawn from all parts of Attica (and, at the City Dionysia, also from abroad) and including the highest civic and religious officials.

The Theatre of Dionysus under the southern slope of the Acropolis, where the two festivals were held, had within living memory undergone a major rebuilding; this project is traditionally associated with the name of Lycurgus, who was the leading figure in Athenian politics and administration from 336 to 324, though recent research (see especially Papastamati-von Moock 2014) shows that it had been begun as early as the 350s and was not fully completed until after 320. Whereas previously – and in the time of Aeschylus, Sophocles, Euripides and Aristophanes – the theatre had been mainly of wooden construction, it was now all of stone; but the basic spaces making up the performing area were much the same as before – the 'dancing-place' (*orchēstra*) in which the chorus performed, and which could also be used by the principals; side-passages (*eisodoi*, later called *parodoi*) for entries from, and exits towards, places at a distance; and a building at the back (still called the *skene*, the 'booth', despite being now a permanent and imposing edifice with a columniated front and projecting wings) representing up to three houses or other interior spaces that played a role in the action. In *Epitrepontes*, as in many other Menandrian plays, only two of the three *skene* doors are in use – doubtless the two lateral doors, one representing the house of Charisios (which is lacking both its owner and his son and heir, until they both come home in the latter part of Act IV), the other that of his friend Chairestratos. Three offstage locations are of importance in the play: the home of Smikrines, Charisios' father-in-law; the pastures and woodlands where Daos the shepherd and Syriskos the charcoal-burner live and work; and the city and market-place (Agora) of Athens, which are assumed to be a considerable way off but within walking distance in an age when men were prepared to walk much further than most would be willing to do today.[17] The first two of these three locations, however, are never mentioned in the same context,[18] so the same *eisodos* can serve for both of them, with the other representing the direction of the city.[19]

Ever since the *skene* was incorporated into the fictive dramatic space (about 460 BC), the only actions and conversations that could normally be presented directly, in any form of Greek drama, were those that took place out of doors. Previously it had been possible to make the audience imagine an indoor setting,[20] and a special-effect device (now known as the *ekkyklēma*; probably a wheeled platform that could be windlassed out of the *skene* door) was created to ensure this option remained available; but Menander only rarely used the *ekkyklema*,[21] and so far as we can tell he did not use it at all in *Epitrepontes*. Consequently, like other Greek dramatists, he will sometimes have a scene take place in the open air which in real life – even life in a climate much more conducive to outdoor living than those of northern Europe – would probably have happened indoors. A case in point is the argument between Smikrines and Pamphile in Act IV of *Epitrepontes*; its opening lines (702–10) are poorly preserved, but there is nothing to suggest that anything was said to explain why the father and daughter have come outside – it is as if Menander assumed that an audience eager to hear what each party had to say, and aware that if the characters stayed indoors they would not be heard, simply would not ask such a question. On the other hand, the convention 'indoors = unseen' is very deftly exploited in regard to Charisios. He remains just offstage, in Chairestratos' house, during three-quarters of the play, is much talked about by others and is never seen. After the end of the Smikrines-Pamphile scene we learn that Charisios had been eavesdropping on the conversation from behind Chairestratos' front door; but we learn that not from Charisios himself but from the slave Onēsimos, and not until, unknown to both, the crucial 'recognition' – the discovery that the baby Daos found in the woods is the child of Charisios and Pamphile – has already been made. And then, finally, after Onesimos has described Charisios' seemingly crazy behaviour in a thirty-line monologue,[22] Charisios himself comes on the scene, vehemently denouncing himself and declaring his determination to stand by Pamphile as she has stood by him. A moment later he will learn that all his troubles are over (just as Pamphile learns that hers are over, shortly after making her declaration of unconditional loyalty to Charisios). In one sense he is the central character of the play; but to the complicated mechanism of its plot he, almost alone of the characters, has made no contribution whatsoever, and he has not even appeared until after the plot has reached its dénouement. Once he

understands the happy outcome, he soon disappears again, into his own
house to join his wife and son; we do not see the reunion, and it is
disputed whether we ever see Charisios again (see Chapter 4).

As in all forms of Greek drama, the performers wore masks
(or rather headpieces which also included a haired or a bald wig as
appropriate); this convention incidentally facilitated both the doubling
of parts by the same actor and the splitting of a single part between
different actors, but it must nevertheless have been possible to identify
at least the principal actor (*prōtagōnistēs*), since there was a competition,
with prizes, for best protagonist. The masks, and also the costumes, gave
clear signals about the stock type to which a character belonged, but in
Menander these signals often prove misleading. The costumes were
much closer in form to those of ordinary life than had been the case in
Old Comedy. Free men and all women, including sex-workers (*hetairai*)
like Habrotonon, wore their clothes long; slaves and cooks were often
more skimpily dressed or otherwise unconventional;[23] but the phallus,
which had been ubiquitous in earlier comedy, was no longer to be seen.

What We Know About *Epitrepontes*, and How We Know It

Epitrepontes means 'men submitting a dispute to the judgement of an arbitrator'. Trial scenes notoriously often make good theatre, and an arbitration scene, with precisely three significant participants, would be particularly well suited to Greek drama; but anyone who came fresh to the play knowing nothing of it but the title would be surprised to learn that the arbitration scene in *Epitrepontes*, far from being pivotal to the play, presents a dispute between two minor characters (one of whom never appears again, while the other makes his final exit early in the next act) and that the arbitrator's verdict is quite soon rendered irrelevant when Onesimos discovers that his master must be the baby's father. The play is named after this scene less because of its importance to the plot than because it is unusual and distinctive (one might compare the Shakespearean title *The Tempest*, which properly describes only the opening scene of the play). And yet the scene does have considerable dramatic significance, both as to plot and character. Had there been no arbitration, or had Daos won his case, he would have retained the trinkets found with the baby, including Charisios' ring, and its parents would never have been identified. Moreover, the audience will have been aware (thanks to the lost divine prologue) that Smikrines is unwittingly deciding the fate of his own grandson.

Our main source of evidence about *Epitrepontes* is the so-called Cairo codex (Figure 1), of the fifth century AD, first published by Gustave Lefebvre in 1907. This famous manuscript, or rather what is left of it (it was taken apart in the sixth century and its leaves used as file covers), contains parts of five plays of Menander (one of which has never been identified and is still known only as the *Fabula Incerta*) and

Figure 1 A page of the Cairo codex, containing part of the arbitration scene of *Epitrepontes* (lines 328–59).

also of the *Demes* of the Old Comic dramatist Eupolis.[1] From *Epitrepontes* it gives us all or part of some 750 lines from Acts II to V, though after the middle of Act III much of its text is very scrappy.

Twelve or thirteen[2] other fragments of different ancient copies are now known, and the play was clearly a very popular one between the second and fifth centuries AD; all the papyri come from this period, nine of them from the single smallish town of Oxyrhynchus. The oldest fragment, now in St Petersburg, was part of the very first ancient text of Menander to be discovered (by Constantin von Tischendorf at Mount Sinai in 1844), but most of the others have become known only quite recently: only four fragments besides the Cairo codex were available in 1972 when Sandbach published the first Oxford Classical Text of Menander. The new fragments often duplicate the Cairo codex and each other (though sometimes they offer new and better readings, and frequently they complete or at least supplement lines which were previously known only in a fragmentary state); but they have also given us parts or glimpses of several scenes and passages which had been thought completely lost. In particular, three overlapping papyri have largely restored to us a crucial phase of the Smikrines-Pamphile scene in Act IV (786–835) of which we previously knew only three lines quoted by a late antique author. Another has preserved maddeningly small fragments (only one line has more than nine letters surviving) of sixty-odd lines from Act I, from which we learn only one thing for certain – that Onesimos and Kariōn, who opened the play, were later joined on stage by Chairestratos. We also now know more about the beginning of Act II leading up to the arbitration scene, about the end of Act III and beginning of Act IV, and a little more about the end of the play, in which Chairestratos, once again, now proves to have had a role. But we still have no clear picture of the opening dialogue between Onesimos and Karion; we still have nothing at all of the delayed divine prologue which most scholars are sure the play must have contained; we still do not know for sure whether there was a subsidiary love interest involving Chairestratos and Habrotonon (or, if there was such a sub-plot, what its outcome was), or whether Habrotonon or Onesimos or both were granted the freedom which the former, but not the latter, had at one time been confident of securing (538–49, 557–62).

There are ten further passages,[3] ranging from a single word up to three lines, quoted from *Epitrepontes* by various authors from Athenaeus (early third century AD) to Photius (ninth century, but certainly using an earlier lexicographical source). They include the opening words of the play (F 1) and a poignant remark by Pamphile at the lowest ebb of her despair ('I was all burned up with weeping', F 8), probably referring to the time when she had to abandon her baby as the only way to save her marriage (and now believing herself to be about to lose her marriage too – but in a minute or two Habrotonon will be giving them both back to her).

The remarkable set of mosaics, probably of the fourth century AD, in the so-called House of the Menander at Mytilene on Lesbos (Charitonides et al. 1970) includes one labelled *Epitrepontōn M^e* (= *Meros*) *B*, i.e. '*Epitrepontes*, Act II' (Figure 2). In the centre, white-haired and with decorated clothing, is *Smeikrinēs* [*sic*]. The other two characters have noticeably darker faces, appropriate to men who have to work outdoors all day in all weathers. The man to Smikrines' left, labelled *Syros*, wears trousers and has his mouth open, suggesting that he is speaking; but Smikrines' head is slightly turned towards the other man, who is labelled *Anthrakeus* ('charcoal-burner') and in front of whom stands a woman, about half his height and breadth, holding a small baby. Whoever inserted the labels, whether it was the maker of the mosaic or (more likely) some earlier artist, has got the identities of the slaves badly confused. The slave

Figure 2 Mosaic from the House of the Menander, Mytilene, Lesbos: *Epitrepontes*, Act II – the arbitration scene. Left to right: Daos (mislabelled Syros), Smikrines, Syriskos (labelled Anthrakeus, 'charcoal-burner'), Syriskos' wife with baby.

currently in possession of the baby, who is destined to prevail in the contest before the arbitrator, is indeed a charcoal-burner, but it is *he*, and not his rival, who is named Syros (more accurately, Syriskos); the loser, a shepherd, is named Daos. Possibly in the first labelled version of this image the possessor of the baby was named as 'Syros the charcoal-burner', and the later artist (if that is not too flattering a term) took these as the designations of separate characters and overlooked the name Daos entirely. These mosaics are late and somewhat degenerate products of an iconographic tradition that probably originated with a set of paintings of scenes from Menander's plays commissioned in Athens not long after his death (Csapo 1999; Green 2010: 93–102; Csapo 2010: 140–67; Nervegna 2013: 122–69).

More general evidence on masks and costume styles comes from a wide variety of artistic representations linked to comedy – vase-paintings (which, however, give out about the time of Menander), monumental reliefs, murals, mosaics, terracotta masks and figurines – and also from an extensive catalogue of masks, and a brief digest of costumes, in the *Onomasticon* of the lexicographer Julius Pollux (second century AD). As sources of evidence on language, style, technique and thought we have (this listing is not exhaustive) the other plays and fragments of Menander, the fragments of other contemporary comic dramatists, the Roman adaptations by Plautus and especially Terence,[4] and the works of intellectuals who taught or influenced Menander, in particular Aristotle (especially his ethical treatises) and Theophrastus (especially his *Characters*, whose rich vein of humour suggests a strong appreciation of comedy).

4

What Happens in *Epitrepontes*

The opening words of *Epitrepontes* have been preserved by an ancient commentator on Aristotle and, in part, by the papyrus Hypothesis:

> In the name of the gods, Onesimos, didn't your young master, who's now taken up with the harp-girl Habrotonon – didn't he just recently get married?

F 1

With remarkable efficiency this sentence of two and a half lines introduces us to a paradoxical and intriguing situation, and to no fewer than five characters. There is the speaker, whom we can identify from other evidence[1] as a cook named Karion (the original audience will have known him for a cook at once, from the knives and other culinary equipment which he or an assistant is carrying). There is the addressee, a slave named Onesimos ('Profitable', a common name for slaves both in comedy and in real life), who will prove to be the first of four slave characters with important roles.[2] There is Onesimos' 'young master' (*trophimos*),[3] whose name, as we will later learn, is Charisios, and whom we will expect to be a major character (though in fact it will be a long time before we even see him on stage). There is his new wife (Pamphile); perhaps (we may suppose) she will remain offstage as young women of citizen status often do in Menander, perhaps she will be passionately angry against her rival (what actually happens is very different). And there is the 'harp-girl' Habrotonon, whom we will (correctly) assume to be, like all young female musicians in New Comedy, a sex-worker with supplementary skills. Cooks in New Comedy are always hired (normally for a day at a time), and our presumption (which will prove only half correct) will be that Charisios has hired Karion for a party of some kind, at which he is enjoying himself with Habrotonon.

But married men, and especially *newly* married men, don't normally in New Comedy disport themselves with *hetairai*. How is it that Charisios is doing so? Despite the new papyrus evidence, the conversation between Onesimos and Karion is impossible to follow in detail, but we can infer fairly accurately, from what we learn in other parts of the play, what the loose-tongued Onesimos must have told the cook – and thereby also told the audience. About six months ago, Charisios married Pamphile, the daughter of the wealthy Smikrines, who brought him a large dowry. What he did not know was that his bride was already pregnant. Five months later, probably while Charisios was away on a business trip, his wife gave birth to a son.[4] With the help of her old nurse Sophronē,[5] she abandoned the baby in the nearby woods (cf. 242), a practice condoned by custom and rarely if ever punished (see Chapter 5). Onesimos somehow or other discovered what had happened, and took an early opportunity of telling his master. Charisios was devastated. He left the marital home to stay next door with his friend Chairestratos, plunged into endless partying, and hired Habrotonon from a pimp (*pornoboskos*, 136) to provide him with further consolation. Today is the third successive day when such a party has been held (cf. 440), but the first time that Karion has been hired to cater it (cf. 382–4). But the audience will have noticed the significance of what Charisios has *not* done: he has not divorced his wife.[6]

At some point Chairestratos comes out of his house and talks with the other two.[7] It is again all but impossible to catch the drift of what is being said, but there are two references to the high-quality wine from the island of Thasos (*Oxyrhynchus Papyrus* 4936 col. ii lines 29, 31), suggesting that Charisios is sparing no expense.[8] Probably Chairestratos warns the others, particularly Onesimos, that Smikrines may well intervene in his daughter's interest; possibly he also gives some indication that Charisios, despite paying a high daily fee for Habrotonon (cf. 136–8), is showing a curious lack of interest in her, and that meanwhile he himself has been captivated by her charms.

All three of the characters on stage eventually go into Chairestratos' house, one of them undoubtedly exiting some time before the others to enable his actor to change mask and costume before reappearing in another role. The consensus of scholars is that the opening scene is followed by a 'delayed prologue' spoken by an omniscient god or goddess[9] who can tell the audience things unknown to any of the human characters. At a minimum, this divinity would reveal two facts: first, that Pamphile's baby has been picked up (perhaps adding 'by a local shepherd') and is being cared for; secondly, that his father is, and will soon be revealed to be, none other than Charisios, who had raped his future wife Pamphile at a celebration of the Tauropolia festival,[10] neither of them knowing who the other was. It does not need to be said that this discovery will make the child legitimate, an Athenian citizen, and eventually Charisios' heir.[11] The deity may have said other things too, but Menander is unlikely to have given much away about the very complex route by which the happy ending will be reached. Unfortunately this prologue, which may have been about fifty lines long,[12] is almost the only substantial section of *Epitrepontes* from which nothing whatever, not even a quotation, has survived.

Our first reasonably intelligible block of text (127–77)[13] is supplied mainly by the Tischendorf leaf now in St Petersburg, with a gap in the middle which is partly filled by Oxyrhynchus Papyrus 4021. It begins with Smikrines soliloquizing about Charisios' extravagance; he seems much more concerned about the dissipation of his dowry than about the desertion of his daughter.[14] And it is likewise revealing when he complains (134–5) that Charisios, 'having received a dowry of four silver talents, has not regarded himself as his wife's servant'. Smikrines, who of course does not know about the baby, is quite entitled to say that Charisios has treated his wife badly, but not that her dowry gives her the right to be the *de facto* master of the household.[15] Chairestratos, who has come outside for reasons that he may have explained in the lost beginning of the scene,[16] is listening to Smikrines (who does not notice him) and making comments 'aside'. Then Habrotonon comes out. Are we going to see some kind of romantic development? Obviously not while Smikrines is around – and anyway she has only come outside to tell Chairestratos that Charisios is waiting for him (142). She has to listen to some disparaging remarks by Smikrines about herself (145–6). The next fourteen lines, mostly preserved (very poorly) only in *Oxyrhynchus Papyrus* 4021, present some puzzles which at present are insoluble. At any rate, Smikrines decides (161–3) to find out more about the situation from his daughter and then consider how to tackle Charisios and get his dowry back (the words 'repaying' and 'the dowry' have survived at the start of lines 153–4). Habrotonon and Chairestratos agree that Charisios must be told about his father-in-law's intentions, and there follows an interesting exchange:

> **Chair.** What a fox! He's turning the home upside down.
> **Habr.** I'd like him to do that to lots of homes!
> **Chair.** Lots?
> **Habr.** Well, the one next door, anyway.
> **Chair.** What, mine?
> **Habr.** Yes, yours!
>
> 165–8

This sounds very much as if Habrotonon is, in Furley's words, 'putting out her "feelers" to Chairestratos'. That is as far as she can go at the moment, since it is Charisios who is her client, and she immediately continues 'Let's go in here to Charisios', and they both go inside, further encouraged to do so by the arrival of 'a crowd of half-drunk young men' whom (says Chairestratos, in words that seem to have signalled the end of Act I in numerous comedies) 'it would be a good idea to get out of the way of'. Meanwhile we, and Chairestratos, have noted Habrotonon's hint. But this subplot will now go to sleep for a long time – and when it awakens, the situation will have been transformed by Habrotonon's pretence that she is the mother of a baby whose father is Charisios.

Now the 'half-drunk young men' – the chorus of the play – enter and perform an interlude, dancing and probably singing too, as they will do in all the other intervals between acts. They have no dramatic function whatever, and during the acts they may have retired to an inconspicuous position; their performances are marked in the script by the single word *khorou*, probably an abbreviation of *khorou melos* 'song of the chorus'.

We can be fairly sure in general terms what must have happened in the early part of Act II, even though hardly a line can be restored in its entirety with any confidence. Onesimos came out and delivered a soliloquy, in which he must have described the impact on Charisios of the news that Smikrines was on the warpath, and explained that he had been instructed to somehow or other get Smikrines out of the way for the moment. This in itself could do no more than buy time, and we do not now know, if indeed Onesimos mentioned the matter at all, how Charisios and his friends meant to use that time; later developments will in any case render irrelevant whatever plans they had. But some spectators may ask themselves why Charisios should want to frustrate Smikrines at all. Smikrines clearly wants to end his daughter's marriage and reclaim her dowry. A husband who discovered that his bride had been carrying (as he thought) another man's child would normally wish to end the marriage anyway. Why doesn't Charisios? Is it because he is unable or unwilling to return the dowry? Hardly: given the circumstances, he would have a good chance of holding on to it on the plea that the marriage had been made under false pretences.[17] We may already have been told, by Onesimos or by the divine prologue-speaker, that Charisios is still fond of his wife and cannot bring himself to cast her off, or at least been given some hints tending in that direction, which will be confirmed when we learn (434–41) that in three days he has not laid a finger on Habrotonon and is now refusing even to recline next to her at table.

Smikrines comes out of Charisios' house and presumably reports what Pamphile has told him about recent events (she may have had to tell a lie or two; if her father asked her why Charisios had left home, she would have had to say that she did not know). He may then have decided to confront Charisios at once; but he will have been intercepted by Onesimos telling him that Charisios has gone off to the city (cf. 577–81). Onesimos then goes inside leaving Smikrines alone to ruminate on Charisios' iniquities. Smikrines is on the point of leaving for town (209) when he stops short on seeing two men and a woman with a baby arriving from the opposite direction; their clothes testify to their humble status (they are in fact all slaves, and one of them, the one with the wife and child, belongs to Chairestratos, for he says 'the master . . . lives here', 214–5). The men are quarrelling, apparently over some property which the second man, who is on his own, is carrying in a closed pouch (cf. 363–4). We will later learn that he is a shepherd named Daos, and the first man is a charcoal-burner named Syriskos.[18] Smikrines can no more avoid fixing his eyes on this scene than the average present-day driver can avoid slowing down to look at an accident site on the other side of a motorway. Suddenly he finds himself directly involved. One of the two men proposes that they ask someone to arbitrate the dispute; the other agrees, saying he doesn't mind who the arbitrator is; and they approach the first man they see. We are at the threshold of the play's most iconic scene, from which it took its name.[19] The more knowledgeable spectators will soon have realized that this scene is modelled on one in Euripides' now lost *Alopē* where a very similar quarrel was arbitrated by a man who, like Smikrines, was actually the grandfather of the baby at the centre of the dispute[20] (see Chapter 8, pp. 75–6). Many will also have guessed that the objects in the pouch will somehow make possible the discovery of the baby's parentage, even before they are reminded by Syriskos (320–43) of famous mythical precedents.

Smikrines is at first impatient with the two men, saying that as manual labourers they ought not to be indulging in litigation, but is persuaded by Syriskos who argues eloquently that it is everyone's duty to ensure that right prevails over wrong (230–6), and after ascertaining that both parties are willing to abide by his decision, he asks Daos to speak first.[21] Daos speaks as follows (240–92):

> I'll go back a bit beyond my dealings with this man, so you can understand the whole thing clearly. About a month ago I was tending my flock in the woods near here, alone by myself, when I found a little baby lying there, with a necklace and other such ornaments . . . I picked it up, took it home and began to look after it. That was my initial decision, but that night I gave thought to the matter, as happens to everyone, and said to myself 'What have I got to do with child-rearing and all its troubles? How will I be able to afford such expense? Why should I have all those worries?' That was how I felt. In the morning I was back with

my flock, when this man came to the same place to saw some stumps –
he's a charcoal-burner, and we already knew each other. We got talking,
and noticing I was looking glum, he said 'What's Daos got on his mind?'
'Why,' I said, 'I've poked my nose where it shouldn't have gone', and told
him the tale, how I'd found and picked up the baby. Before I'd even
finished he was beseeching me, ending every sentence with 'so may
good things befall you, Daos'. 'Give me the baby – so may you be happy,
so may you be free. I've got a wife, she had a baby but it died' – meaning
that woman that's holding the baby now ... He spent the whole day
going on like that, begging and begging till I agreed and made a promise.
I gave it to him, and he went off praying for millionfold blessings on me.
When he took it, he kissed both my hands ... Off he went, and now he's
met me again and suddenly demands that I hand over the stuff that was
left with the baby – small worthless trinkets they were – and says I'm
cheating him by not doing so and claiming the right to keep them
myself. I say he should be grateful for the share he got when he begged
for it. If I didn't give him the whole lot, that doesn't give him the right to
interrogate me about it. If we'd found the stuff while walking together so
that it was a joint treasure-trove, then I suppose we'd have split it. But I
was the sole finder; you weren't even there, and yet you think that you
should have the lot and me nothing at all. The bottom line is: I gave you
part of what belonged to me. If you're happy with that, keep it. If you're
not, if you've changed your mind, give it back, and you'll not have done
me wrong or cheated me. But to have the lot, half by my consent and
half by force – no, you can't. I have said what I have to say.

240–92

Daos treats this purely as a property dispute, and his language
consistently implies that the baby too is a piece of property. And if the
'ornaments' are of such little value, why is he so determined to have
them back? Syriskos takes a very different line (294–352). He begins
what has been described as 'perhaps the best forensic speech in all
surviving comedy' (Buis 2014: 336) admitting all the facts as alleged by
Daos are true, and continues:

Another shepherd, one of this man's fellow-workers that he'd talked to,
told me that he'd found some ornaments with the baby. Sir, their owner

is here in person to claim them. (Wife, give me the baby.) He claims
from you, Daos, the necklace and the other identification tokens. He
says they were left with him for his adornment, not for your sustenance.

                                                                    299–305

Brilliant rhetoric: the baby is repeatedly 'he' (*houtos* or *houtosi*), not 'it'
(*auto*) as Daos had called him (250), the ornaments are 'identification
tokens' (*gnōrismata*) – anticipating an argument that will be fully developed
later – and they are being claimed not by Syriskos but by the baby.

And I as his guardian – you made me that by giving him to me – join
myself to his demand. Now, sir, you must decide, it seems to me,
whether this jewellery, or whatever it is, should be kept for the
child until he grows up, according to the wish of the mother who gave
it him – whoever *she* was – or whether the man who robbed him
should keep it just because he was the first to find someone else's
property ... I come now to speak on his behalf, making no personal
demand whatever for myself. 'Shared treasure-trove', you say? You can't
talk about finding treasure when there's a person who has been
wronged. That's not finding, it's stealing. And look at it this way, father.[22]
Perhaps this boy is above our station. If he grows up among labourers
he will despise them, soar to the heights of his own birthright and
embark on ventures worthy of a man of rank like lion-hunting or feats
of arms or competitive athletics. You've seen the tragedies, I know, and
you're aware of all this. That Neleus and Pelias[23] were found by an old
goatherd, wearing a leather jerkin just like mine, but when he realized
that they were his superiors he told the story of how he had found
them and picked them up, and he gave them each a little pouch of
identification tokens, from which they learned all about themselves,
and from goatherds they became kings. If Daos had taken those tokens
and sold them to enrich himself by twelve drachmas, these great,
nobly-born men would have remained in obscurity all their lives. It's
not fair, father, that I should be rearing him physically to manhood
while Daos has scattered his hopes of freedom to the winds. By means
of recognition tokens a man has avoided marrying his sister,[24]
another met and rescued his mother,[25] a third saved his brother.[26]
Nature makes life precarious for everyone, father, and one must protect

it by forethought, seeing well in advance the ways to make this possible. 'Give it back', he says, 'if you're dissatisfied', and he thinks that's a strong and relevant argument. It's not fair, when you've got to hand back something that belongs to him, to try and take *him* as well, so that you can be safe in your villainy again, even now that Fortune has preserved some of his property!

306–51

Smikrines immediately announces his decision. The objects left with the baby belong to the baby, and the baby belongs to 'the man who came to his aid and acted against you [Daos] when you tried to cheat him' (356–7). It is of course ironic that Smikrines, of all people, should decide against Daos because Daos was more concerned with his own net worth than with human kindness, but he may be the sort of person who has a well-developed sense of justice in all matters except those which affect his own interests. Daos, bitterly protesting, is made to hand over the pouch and its contents; Smikrines waits until this has been done, and then leaves for town. Daos leaves also. Syriskos, left alone with his wife, begins to take an inventory of the objects in the pouch.

At this point Onesimos comes outside, complaining about the slow service being provided by the cook. Nosy fellow that he is, he cannot help listening to Syriskos' careful description of each item. The fourth item is a highly distinctive ring, inscribed with the maker's name,[27] which Onesimos at once realizes is one that had been lost some time ago by his master, Charisios. Syriskos is very angry ('They're baby's, not mine!', 403), but realizing that they are both in any case bound for Chairestratos' house he eventually agrees to let Onesimos keep the ring for the time being.

Some confusion has been caused by Onesimos' statement that as guests are arriving, 'perhaps it isn't a good time to tell master about it now – rather do it tomorrow' (411–13), followed by his appearance at the beginning of the next act (Act III) saying that he's started 'more than five times' to take the ring and show it to his master, and each time has funked it. Taken together, these passages seem to imply that a day has passed between Acts II and III. But it is not like Menander to fail to make a matter like this crystal clear, and there are strong counter-arguments, of which the most important are these:

1. In the supposed interval of twenty-four hours, nothing whatever has happened except that Onesimos has repeatedly tried and failed to pluck up courage to show the ring to Charisios.
2. It would have to be assumed that Smikrines had stayed in the city overnight, and likewise that Karion had stayed at Chairestratos' house overnight and, contrary to New Comic convention, had catered at least three meals (two lunches and one dinner).
3. At the end of Act II the guests for a lunch party are still arriving (412); at the beginning of Act III a lunch party has reached the stage of drunken rowdiness, with some guests trying to lay hands on Habrotonon who has been hired for the exclusive benefit of Charisios, not for the company (430–1). The natural inference, supported by the general practice of New Comedy, is that these two lunch parties are one and the same.
4. Onesimos at 435–6 entertains, and dismisses, the idea of returning the ring to 'the man I got it from just now'; if a day has passed since Syriskos handed him the ring, it would be both more natural for Onesimos and more convenient for Menander if Onesimos were to say he had received the ring 'yesterday'.

As Geoffrey Arnott explains (1987: 25–7), in New Comedy 'tomorrow' is normally a day that never comes, because by the end of today the action of the play will be over. This is all the more true in the case of Syriskos, who will have to be back at work tomorrow (379–80). So Onesimos, who is frightened to show the ring to Charisios at all (cf. 419–22), promises to do so at a time when he hopes Syriskos will not be there to force him to keep the promise. But Syriskos calls his bluff by saying 'I'll wait', and Onesimos knows he has no alternative but to perform this unwelcome duty. He explains his nervousness in a short soliloquy (419–29). Both he and the audience understand the significance of the ring, though it will not be spelt out until 446–57. The ring was left with the baby when it was exposed; therefore it must have been in the possession of the baby's mother. The only obvious way in which it could have come into her possession would be if Charisios had raped her[28] and in the struggle she had either pulled off the ring or it had dropped off and she had picked it up. Either way, it identifies Charisios as the baby's father. Charisios is already angry with Onesimos for telling him about Pamphile's baby. That is very revealing: Charisios *would rather not have known* that his wife had given birth to a child who presumably could not be his, and to 'stir another ingredient into the mix' (428) will probably make things even worse for him.

Habrotonon now comes outside, apparently to escape the unwelcome attentions of some men at the party. Not those of Charisios, though. She cannot understand his behaviour: 'I expected he'd love me, but the man seems to hate me prodigiously' (432–3); he has paid a large sum to hire her, and yet after more than two days she is still, so far as he is concerned, *virgo intacta!*[29] We can hardly doubt it now: Charisios still loves his wife, loves her so strongly that when he seeks consolation with another woman he finds he cannot bear even to touch her, so strongly that he would like nothing more than to pretend that Pamphile's baby had never existed. And, as Onesimos perceives, that would be possible. If Smikrines can be prevented from breaking up the marriage, and if Charisios can master his conflicting emotions and return to his wife, they might seek to keep their secret safe by causing Onesimos to 'disappear' (427).[30]

At this point Syriskos comes out, looking for Onesimos. He demands the ring back; Onesimos explains that it belongs to his master, who lost it at the Tauropolia 'when there was an all-night party of women' (451–2). He must have committed a rape, and be the father of the baby (who is presently being cared for by Syriskos' wife). Syriskos lets him keep the ring for the time being, and leaves, having business in the city. He will not be seen again. His wife and the baby remain in Chairestratos' house.

Habrotonon has overheard this conversation. She has grown fond of the baby – and she remembers something that happened at last year's Tauropolia (475–92). She was providing music for a group of unmarried girls (she was a virgin herself then, she says), and one of them was indeed the victim of a rape – at any rate she wandered off on her own and then rushed back, crying, tearing her hair, and with her clothes torn to rags. She didn't know who the girl was, but she would recognize her if she saw her again; the girl was very beautiful, and said to come from a rich family.

Onesimos naturally thinks that the first thing to do is to identify the victim and thus establish the exact parentage of the baby. But Habrotonon points out that they cannot yet be certain that Charisios is the baby's father: he might have given the ring to someone else in a variety of scenarios of business or gambling (502–7). It is essential to confirm his paternity first; otherwise it will not be possible to help the mother or the baby. And Habrotonon has a brilliant idea to achieve this: she will take the ring, and the baby, and *pretend to be the rape victim herself.* If Charisios is startled into a confession, 'we can then look for the girl at our leisure' (537–8).

Onesimos has perceived that Habrotonon is not being entirely altruistic: she stands to gain her freedom, for Charisios will not want his son to grow up a slave.[31] What is more, it is possible that once she has secured her freedom as Charisios' permanent partner (*pallakē*) she will drop the rest of the scheme, and drop Onesimos too; her reaction ('Why should I do that? Do you think I've a passionate desire for motherhood? Just let me be free, ye gods; may I have that as my reward!') apparently convinces him sufficiently, and he gives the ring to Habrotonon who takes it inside. Onesimos, left alone, reflects that *he* is not that clever, and not likely to be that lucky.[32] He also reflects that things are looking bad for Pamphile: if the baby's mother is of citizen birth, as now seems likely, Charisios will want to divorce Pamphile and marry her. But he consoles himself with the thought that whatever happens, this time it won't be his fault (572–3). Onesimos now sees Smikrines returning from town, looking angry; he guesses that Smikrines has discovered that Onesimos had lied to him, and he makes himself scarce.

The rest of Act III (583–701) is poorly preserved (though recent discoveries have considerably improved our knowledge of the last part, from 655 onwards). We cannot of course see Habrotonon carrying out her plan, but only hear what other people say about it.

Smikrines, while in town, appears to have learned a good deal about Charisios' current lifestyle, not all of it necessarily accurate; we can catch words like 'wastrel' (*asōtos*), 'drinking', 'harp-girl', 'gambling perhaps', and his monologue ends 'farewell to him' (602), i.e. in effect 'good riddance to him'. Then out comes Karion, complaining (to no one in particular) that the lunch party is breaking up[33] (which probably means that he won't be paid); we cannot follow what else he said, but he must have said enough to make Smikrines suspect that Habrotonon has had a baby of which Charisios is the father.[34] Karion's last surviving word is 'let's go', and he and his assistant (who may be named Simias) depart.

The next character to appear is Chairestratos (he is addressed at 660, and his abbreviated name appears in the Cairo codex at 692). In the present state of the text, it is only at the very end of the scene that we learn why he has come out of his house:

> It's all up with me, as far as I can see . . . I must go [to] the job to which I've been assigned.
>
> 699–701

We can be certain that this somehow arises from what Habrotonon has done. We may note, too, that when Chairestratos eventually returns (979–89), he speaks about Habrotonon and about his duty to be a loyal friend to Charisios. There can be little doubt that Arnott's interpretation of his position is correct. Charisios has fallen for Habrotonon's deception and believes that she is the girl he raped, and the mother of his child. As she anticipated, he has decided it is his duty to set her free, and probably to take her as his *pallakē*,[35] and he has accordingly sent his friend to buy her from her owner, a *pornoboskos* presumably living in the city (Charisios, of course, providing the money for the purchase – which will not be cheap).[36] Through no fault of his own Chairestratos thus sees his hopes of a relationship with Habrotonon totally extinguished.

And what is more, he has to listen to a tirade of abuse from Smikrines, directed mainly at Charisios. It is not clear exactly when the two men become aware of each other's presence, but when they do, Smikrines does almost all the talking, denouncing Charisios' supposed immorality in wildly exaggerated terms[37] and declaring his intention of terminating the marriage[38] (657–9, 689–92; cf. 662) and (as he typically adds) reclaiming his dowry (688). Chairestratos, after his opening speech of five or six lines (631–6), makes only a few ineffective interventions, primarily in defence of his friend. At 662–3 he may say that Smikrines' intention of taking his daughter away is 'unworthy of us and of you'; when Smikrines repeats his determination to do so he pleads 'don't, not yet' (688); and when Smikrines then says that Pamphile won't stay in that house another hour 'or else I'm an illegal immigrant',[39] Chairestratos assures him that that is not what Charisios thinks of his in-laws.[40]

All in vain. Having ranted almost non-stop for sixty lines (637–96),[41] Smikrines abruptly turns on his heel and goes into his son-in-law's house, leaving Chairestratos to depart on his unwelcome mission to town.

Habrotonon's well-meaning and brilliant scheme thus appears to have had disastrous consequences. The marriage of Pamphile and Charisios, which the husband had been so reluctant to break, is apparently at an end. Habrotonon is lost to Chairestratos, who is in love with her; instead she will become, at least until further notice, the *pallake* of Charisios, who will certainly treat her fairly and decently but is unlikely to have any passionate feelings in her direction. And unless Habrotonon and Onesimos can somehow identify the baby's mother, the infant, having only one parent a citizen, will grow up a *metoikos* or resident alien, without the right to vote, to hold either state or local office, to sit on a jury, or to own any real estate, even his own home.[42] We are about to begin Act IV, and experienced Menander watchers would know that by the end of Act IV the main issue of a play is normally settled.[43] We know what the settlement will be; we were told, much earlier, by a god. But how on earth is it to be reached, in the space of one act?

One key to the solution appears right at the start of Act IV: it quickly becomes evident that Pamphile does not want to give up on the marriage. As we probably expected, the act begins with Smikrines leading her out of the marital home,[44] but it will be obvious that she is reluctant to go – perhaps she is even being half-dragged out, and her first words (705–6) 'Daddy, what's all this? . . . Are you going to be my guardian (*kyrios*) for ever?', and a moment later (713–4) 'If you try to save me without gaining my consent, you'll not be treating me as a daughter but as a slave.'[45] This is enough to start Smikrines off on another rant against Charisios, much of which is lost, but whose length can be estimated (from the page length of the Cairo codex) at about 84 lines. In the surviving portions Pamphile does not say a word. Smikrines starts by saying that if Pamphile stays with Charisios, he will get all the pleasure and she will get none (720); he ends by arguing that Habrotonon, as a *hetaira*, will know the best ways to win Charisios' heart, and will in the end be more truly his wife, in fact if not in law, than Pamphile is (790–6). A short passage has survived from the middle of the speech (749–55) in which Smikrines first argues that Charisios is sure to ruin himself by trying to keep up two families, and then paints a picture of Pamphile sitting waiting all night without her supper[46] while Charisios is carousing with his floozie. It is hard to deny that if the facts are as Smikrines believes them to be, the prudential arguments for ending the marriage are overwhelming.[47]

But Pamphile will have none of them. Much of her speech in reply is now known from the Michigan papyrus and two Oxyrhynchus ones.[48] She expresses the utmost respect for her father, and then defies him totally. Her language is at first rather obscure, probably because there are things about her past that she needs to conceal from her father (see Furley 2014a: 37), but presently two arguments emerge clearly. One is (816–21) that she married Charisios to be 'his partner in life' and share *all* his fortunes, not only his good fortunes; if he has 'stumbled', that is no reason for abandoning him. The other (824–29) is that her father, who will certainly marry her off again as soon as he can, cannot possibly guarantee that her second marriage will be any better than her first. Come what may, even if Habrotonon contrives to get her thrown out, she will remain loyal to Charisios (829–30).

Thirty-seven lines into Pamphile's speech, our sources give out, but it cannot have lasted much longer. Smikrines apparently admitted defeat for the time being and left, probably making it clear that he would be back and would bring Pamphile's old nurse, Sophrone, to make a final attempt to persuade her. We may well recall that Sophrone had been responsible for exposing the baby, and wonder whether she will now be the instrument for identifying it. (She will not.)

Pamphile is left alone with her sorrows. She recalls a time when she cried her eyes out (F 8) – either after the rape, or when her baby was exposed – and no doubt expects that another such moment awaits her shortly. Then Habrotonon comes out with the baby; it too has been crying, and she thinks it needs fresh air and a cuddle.[49] For a few moments the two women do not notice each other, as Pamphile laments 'Which of the gods will take pity on me?' (855) and Habrotonon wonders aloud 'Baby darling, when will you see your mother?' (856). Then Pamphile says *poreusomai* 'I'll go' and turns to go – where? Back into Charisios' house? To Chairestratos' house, to seek a reconciliation with her husband? Or away to her father's, surrendering to what seems like the inevitable? Probably we never learn, even on stage; it is quite likely that this is only the first word of a sentence that is never completed.[50] For Habrotonon has suddenly had a feeling that she has seen this young woman before:

Habr.   Lady, wait a moment!
Pam.   Are you calling me?
Habr.   Yes. Look at me straight.
Pam.   What, do you know me, lady?
Habr.   (*aside*) She's the very one that I saw! (*To Pamphile*) Hello, darling!
Pam.   (*puzzled*) Who are you?
Habr.   Give me your hand. [*Pamphile ignores her outstretched hand.*] Tell me, sweetie, did you go to a party at the Tauropolia last year? [*A few words missing*]
Pam.   (*who has been examining the baby's clothes*) Tell me, lady, where did you get this baby from?
Habr.   Darling, do you recognize something of his? Lady, don't be frightened of me!
Pam.   Aren't you its mother?

Habr.   I pretended to be – not meaning to cheat the real mother, but to gain time to find her. Now I have! I see you in front of me, the same girl I saw back then.

Pam.   But who's the father?

Habr.   Charisios.

Pam.   Darling, are you certain of that?

Habr.   Absolutely. But aren't you the newly-married lady from in there [*gesturing towards Charisios' house*]?

Pam.   Yes, I am.

Habr.   Happy lady, some god has taken pity on you both![51]

858–73

At this point a noise from the door of Chairestratos' house warns the pair that someone is coming out, and they withdraw into Pamphile's house where Habrotonon says she will tell her the whole story.

The two women now know the truth about the baby, but there are three important characters to whom it is still unknown: Charisios, Chairestratos and Smikrines. The enlightening of these three will occupy much of the rest of the play. Only one of the three, Charisios, is at present in the vicinity – the character about whom so much has been said, but whom we have never yet seen. And we still do not see him; it is Onesimos who appears – to talk about Charisios.

'He's half mad, by Apollo. He's mad. He's really gone mad. By all the gods, he's mad.' That is how Onesimos begins (878–9). Apparently Charisios was listening at the door to the whole argument between Pamphile and her father, and was dumbstruck by the loyalty she showed him, which he felt he deserved so little. Onesimos reports how he condemned himself:

Accursed that I am! I'd done the same thing myself and become the father of a bastard child, and I didn't have, and didn't give her, any degree of forgiveness when she suffered the same misfortune. I'm a heartless barbarian!

894–9

Onesimos is desperate to keep out of Charisios' way, for his own safety. Having been responsible for telling Charisios about Pamphile's baby in the first place, he fears that Charisios, in his present mood, may lash out and even kill him (902–3). He hears a noise at the door, assumes rightly that Charisios is coming out, and takes refuge in the only place available, Charisios' own house.[52]

And now Charisios himself appears on stage for the first time. He condemns himself eloquently, though he continues to apply the same term 'misfortune' (*atukhēma*) both to Pamphile and to himself, as if he considered himself no more guilty of actual wrongdoing than she was. He decides, at any rate, that he will reciprocate her loyalty. When Smikrines comes back, Charisios will be there to get rid of him:

> 'Stop troubling me, Smikrines. My wife isn't leaving me. Why are you badgering Pamphile and trying to coerce[53] her?'
>
> 929–31

Logically, the next thing Charisios should do is return to his own home – where he would be amazed to find his wife in intimate and friendly conversation with Habrotonon. But before he can do so, he will be rewarded beyond belief for his repentance.

Onesimos has meanwhile, of course, learned the truth from Pamphile and Habrotonon, and now comes outside, somewhat hesitantly, intending to inform his master. Charisios reacts with irritation, and Onesimos begs Habrotonon not to 'leave [him] in the lurch'. She duly joins him (941) and eases things for him by making an important confession: 'the baby wasn't mine' (944). Charisios is still angry with Onesimos for having taken part in deceiving his master (950–2), and Habrotonon sees that it is time to let him fully into the secret. Miraculously, the next six or seven lines are just well enough preserved in the Cairo codex to enable us to appreciate this climactic moment:

> **Habr.** Don't start fighting, sweetheart. The baby's mother is your lawful wedded wife, no one else!
> **Char.** If only!
> **Habr.** By the love of Demeter, it's true.
> **Char.** What's this tale you're telling?
> **Habr.** What tale? The truth!

Char. *(puzzled)* The baby's Pamphile's? But it was mine![54]
Habr. Hers and yours too!
Char. *Pamphile's?* *(As realization dawns)* Habrotonon, I beg you, don't give me false hope!

952–8

At this point the Cairo codex gives out again, but a little later (970–2) we can glimpse Habrotonon explaining why she pretended to be the baby's mother and Charisios accepting that she did the right thing. Act IV ends shortly afterwards: Charisios will go into his own house for a joyful reunion with his wife; Onesimos will follow his master; Habrotonon will tactfully return to Chairestratos' house.

It is typical of Menander to resolve the main issue of a play by the end of Act IV while leaving important secondary business to be cleared up in Act V.[55] In this play the unfinished business relates to Chairestratos and Smikrines. The first half of Act V, though badly preserved, seems to be mainly concerned with Chairestratos. As we have seen, he departed at the end of Act III, probably making for the city to purchase Habrotonon from her owner on Charisios' behalf. He returns now, admonishing himself that he must behave as a loyal friend to Charisios and not even 'look at' Habrotonon any more (987). Two lines later the Cairo codex shuts down almost completely: of the next 70-odd lines only two have more than nine letters surviving, and nearly half are wholly lost. We do, however, have the last two lines of the scene:

He wouldn't have been able to keep his hands off a girl like that, I know that for sure – but *I* will!

1060–1

Who is the speaker here, and what has happened? Thanks to Chairestratos' purchase, Charisios has become the owner of Habrotonon. But in the new situation, she is an embarrassment. It is impossible for him to keep her as a slave, and it would be monstrous to sell her when he knows that he owes to her his new-found happiness. Charisios' only obvious remaining option is to set her free, and thus she will achieve, by an unexpected route,[56] the goal she was aiming at (538–49). Once she is a free woman, Chairestratos will undoubtedly make her an offer; she had probably perceived his interest long before (166–8) and, having also had the opportunity to observe his character, would be happy to accept. The speaker of 1060–1, then, is Charisios. If *he* had taken Habrotonon as a *pallake*, he would always have had to look over his shoulder at Chairestratos; Chairestratos, on the other hand, need have no fear of *him* – because he is not in love with Habrotonon, and (as has become increasingly obvious) *is* in love with his wife.

What, then, happened, dramatically speaking, between 989 and 1060? The meagre textual remains give little help. From 1004 to 1020 the presence of short horizontal strokes (*paragraphoi*) at the beginning of certain lines shows that two characters (at least) are in dialogue; the first line (1004) begins with 'he's gone', which one would expect to refer to Charisios. At 1021 there appears in the margin the abbreviated name of Onesimos; this may or may not indicate that the speech to which it is attached is his first in the scene. Some time later (1040) a line ends with the name Habrotonon; on the two previous occasions when her name has ended a line (157, 535) it was a vocative, addressed to her. Twice (1020, 1052) there appear what seem to be forms of the verb *exapatân* 'deceive', which suggests the presence of Charisios, the only person (aside from Smikrines, who has not yet arrived) who could claim to have been a victim of deception. And at 1055 somebody agrees to a request.

That seems to suggest that we need in this scene Chairestratos, Onesimos, Habrotonon and Charisios. But we cannot have four persons on stage at one time unless one of them is completely silent. Menander is shortly going to be playing that game with the old nurse Sophrone, and the effectiveness of that manoeuvre would be diminished if it had already been performed just previously. And Habrotonon appears not to be present at 1021, when in reply to a reference (by Charisios?) to her deception, Onesimos speaks of someone having 'kept safe' someone or something. Nor does the mention of her at 1040 require her presence, any more than did the mention of her name in the second line of the play (F 1). What *would* require her presence is her formal manumission, but we need not suppose that this takes place on stage: Charisios can simply make a present of Habrotonon to Chairestratos, who can then set her free as and when he wishes. The effect on Charisios will be the same: either way, he has paid out a large sum of money for no gain. One might possibly see this as the penalty he indirectly pays for the original rape.[57]

A scenario like the following may thus be envisaged. After his monologue, Chairestratos' obvious next move would be to report to Charisios that he had successfully performed his mission. He would expect to find Charisios where he had left him, in his (Chairestratos') own house. But a moment after he goes inside he is out again, having discovered that Charisios is no longer there. Chairestratos does not quite know what to do, but at this point Charisios comes out, perhaps looking for Chairestratos to whom he needs to explain the new situation. When he has done so, there will quickly arise the question of what can now be done about Habrotonon. Charisios may think she deserves punishment for deceiving him; but Onesimos (who has come out at some point) reminds him that she has done as much as anyone to ensure that the baby was restored to his true parents and the family reunited. We do not know how the discussion then proceeded, but eventually Chairestratos must have made bold to request that Habrotonon be made over to him, and to this, after some further struggles, Charisios agrees (1057). Chairestratos will now at last go into his own house to join Habrotonon, who arrived in that house as a hired slave-prostitute and will now stay there permanently (or at least until it is time for Chairestratos to marry) as a live-in partner. Onesimos probably also exits, but Charisios will linger (for the space of five to seven lines) to reflect on what has happened and, not less important, to give time for one of the other actors to put on the mask and costume of Smikrines (the latter perhaps over the top of his previous costume) and get down to the appropriate *eisodos*.

Smikrines enters with Sophrone, who has evidently had a lot to say before this moment but will not say a word when on stage. She has apparently accepted that Pamphile's marriage had proved a failure (though unlike Smikrines, she knew what had caused the failure), but she thinks Smikrines ought to secure her consent to ending it (1070) rather than taking her away willy-nilly as he means to do (1068). Smikrines is furious at her presumption, and threatens to break her head or drown her (1062–3, 1072–3). He knocks at his son-in-law's door (which is bolted, no doubt for the first time in the play: 1075–6), doubtless expecting Pamphile to answer, but to his astonishment it is Onesimos who comes to the door. 'Ah,' he says, 'it's that sourpuss Smikrines, come for his dowry and his daughter' (which accurately reflects Smikrines' own priorities, cf. 1065–7), and he continues to enjoy himself at Smikrines' expense for more than fifty lines (1078–1130), giving him a long moral-theological lecture before suddenly inviting him to come in and greet his grandson (1112–3). He then drops hints which he knows Sophrone will understand and Smikrines will not ('at the Tauropolia, my master found her when she'd got separated from the dancing group … but now there's been a recognition and everything's all right', 1118–22), and like Syriskos he can quote tragedy – a passage from Euripides' lost *Auge*,[58] referring to the rape of Auge by Heracles which resulted in the birth of Telephus:

> ''Twas Nature willed it, who cares naught for laws;
> For this was woman made.'

> 1123–4

By this point Sophrone, though still silent, is dancing for joy, and Smikrines is angrier than ever ('you know damn fine what this fellow's talking about', 1126–8). But now he is beginning himself to have some inkling of the truth. His first reaction is that it is appalling (1129), but Onesimos replies that there has never been any greater stroke of good fortune.

Here the Cairo codex ends, but the Michigan papyrus gives us a few extra lines (1133–8). 'If you're telling the truth', Smikrines apparently says, 'the baby must be the child of Charisios and his wedded wife' – and that probably means that he has lost the legal right to reclaim his daughter (and, of course, his dowry) without her consent. Before he can grumble about this, however, Chairestratos comes out of the other house, and some hard words appear to go to and fro between him and

Smikrines (we wryly observe that the promised confrontation between Smikrines and Charisios has not happened). The play, though, cannot have ended on that note, with Smikrines still estranged from his daughter and grandson; perhaps, as Arnott supposed, Chairestratos, with the authority that comes from having no axe to grind, persuaded Smikrines to make peace with Charisios. Menander's plays usually end with a processional *exodos* with garlands and torches, including an appeal for applause and a prayer for victory in the dramatic competition. If *Epitrepontes* ended in this way, one would expect Charisios to be present, and since Smikrines is present too, one would also expect some words of reconciliation to pass between them; but this could only happen if the other speaking character, Onesimos, was removed from the scene. This could be managed, for example, in the following way. Chairestratos asks Onesimos to fetch Charisios from his house,[59] and while waiting for his appearance (delayed slightly by the need for a change of mask and costume) persuades a shaken Smikrines to end his enmity with Charisios, adding perhaps an assurance that Charisios had never been the lover of Habrotonon and will henceforth be truly and exclusively devoted to his wife. Charisios then comes out (with or without Onesimos, who if present will not speak), and he and Smikrines bury the hatchet. Then, or perhaps at an earlier moment, Chairestratos proposes a sacrifice to some appropriate god in honour of the arrival of an heir to both Charisios' and Smikrines' families, and calls for garlands and torches to set up the traditional finale.

Rape, Marriage, Legitimacy, Citizenship and Child Exposure

To the modern western mind it is almost incomprehensible that Pamphile should be overjoyed, as she obviously is, to discover that her husband – to whom she has just declared herself unconditionally loyal, despite his supposed infidelity and her father's determination to break up the marriage – is none other than the stranger who raped her one night a year ago, and that Habrotonon should be equally delighted to have been largely responsible for this discovery. We would have expected them both to be appalled and enraged; we would have expected Pamphile to see at once that her father was right and that Charisios was no fit husband for her, to leave the marital home forthwith, to get herself formally divorced as soon as possible,[1] and to press for a prosecution. Instead, both she and Habrotonon evidently consider that all her problems have been miraculously solved, and that some god (as Habrotonon says) has taken pity on her *and Charisios* (for Habrotonon uses the plural pronoun *humas*).

There is nothing unusual about this, so far as New Comedy is concerned. Numerous dramas in the genre, both Greek and Roman, deal with the consequences of a rape,[2] and never once do they include the actual punishment of the perpetrator; on the contrary, he always ends up married to his victim, and the worst that happens to him is that he is given a reduced (or no) dowry or, as in *Epitrepontes*, suffers financially in some other way.[3] All this in addition to what we may well consider the atrocious insensitivity of treating rape as a mere plot device in a *comic* drama. By contrast, *consensual* sexual relationships between unmarried male and female citizens are in New Comedy non-existent.

It is not as though Athenian law did not regard rape as a serious crime[4] – provided, that is, that the victim was neither the wife nor the slave of the perpetrator. Rape was the paradigm case of the crime of *hybris*[5] (perhaps best translated as 'degrading treatment'), and the punishment of *hybris* was decided by the trial jury making a forced choice between the penalty proposed by the prosecutor and that proposed by the convicted defendant – so that it could be, and sometimes was, punished by death if the prosecutor demanded this and the jury agreed with him.[6] And characters in Menander can express similar attitudes. In *Dyskolos* the struggling young farmer Gorgias learns that another young man – a rich city lad, to judge by his clothes – has been seen talking to his (Gorgias') sister and fetching water for her. Gorgias is furious, and when the young man, Sostratos, returns to the area, Gorgias treats him to a long moral lecture (*Dyskolos* 271–87); Sostratos does not understand what he has done to earn such a rebuke, and Gorgias tells him:

> In my opinion you've set yourself to do an evil deed, thinking you can induce a free girl to go astray, or else awaiting an opportunity to commit a crime that deserves death many times over.
>
> 289–93

Since the first of the two 'evil deeds' is plainly seduction, the second must be rape.[7] But consider the situation of an unmarried young woman who becomes a rape victim (in Menander rape victims always are unmarried at the time of the offence). What can she or her family do? If the perpetrator is identifiable (as in *Samia*), they can of course prosecute him. But if they do so, they are advertising the fact that the woman is no longer a virgin, and running a grave risk of rendering her unmarriageable, particularly if the rapist, his family and his friends choose to retaliate by blackening her character. The one sure way to avoid this risk is to marry her as quickly as possible to the rapist himself;[8] all those involved will then become sharers of a secret which none of them can divulge without harming themselves. In *Samia* this plan is quickly agreed between the rapist, Moschion, and the victim's mother (we are not told whether the victim herself was consulted), though complications arise because Nikeratos, the father of the prospective bride, who alone could authorize the marriage, is abroad on business and in any case has a fierce and unpredictable temper.

If the rapist cannot be identified, a prosecution is of course impossible. Either the victim will become pregnant, or she will not. In New Comedy she always does, but it seems to be assumed that she will be able to conceal her pregnancy for most of its duration,[9] perhaps with the connivance of a loyal servant who may be able to arrange for the child, when born, to be brought up in another household. Meanwhile the child's real mother may well have had a marriage arranged for her. In a marriage which takes place under these circumstances, the husband always providentially proves in the end to be the same man who committed the rape. For this is the only way in which the child can be the legitimate son of his true father, have an assured status as a citizen, or even be sure (the gods willing) of surviving early infancy without being abandoned, or 'exposed' (*ektheis*) as the ancient and modern euphemism has it, to a fate which is uncertain but is most likely to be either death or slavery.[10]

Legitimacy, citizenship, child exposure: three Athenian social institutions whose principles are presupposed by the plot of *Epitrepontes*. Let us begin with citizenship. Except by a special decree of the citizen assembly, no one could be a citizen who was not the child of two citizen parents.[11] Children would be admitted to the father's phratry (a religious 'brotherhood', membership of which was hereditary) in their first year,[12] and, if male, to membership of his deme (see p. 1) on coming of age at eighteen, and both these groups were expected to satisfy themselves that candidates for membership met the birth qualification; at the phratry induction the father (or guardian, if the father was dead) had to take an oath to this effect. A child whose father was not known, or a child whose mother was not of citizen status, even if he had been born in Attica and never set foot outside its borders, was no more than a resident alien (*metoikos*, whose literal meaning is probably 'one who dwells among us'), and if he attempted to exercise any of the rights of a citizen (such as speaking or voting in the assembly, or serving on a jury) he could be prosecuted and, if convicted, sold as a slave. Every baby who is born shortly before, or (as in *Georgos*) actually during, the action of a Menandrian play either dies (like Syriskos' baby in *Epitrepontes* and probably Chrysis' baby in *Samia*) or else proves in the end to be a citizen – and a male citizen at that, for the babies that survive are all boys. The baby whose fate is central to *Epitrepontes* will at best be a *metoikos*, and may be a slave (cf. 469),[13] unless he can be shown to be the child of a citizen father and a citizen mother.

It is now generally accepted that a further qualification for citizenship was *legitimate* birth:[14] one must not only be the child of two citizen parents, but of two citizen parents 'married according to the law' (a phrase included in the oath taken by the father at a child's induction to the phratry: [Demosthenes] 59.60). The same rule certainly applied to inheritance: an illegitimate child (*nothos*) could not be his father's heir, nor could he be legally adopted into another family.[15] Many of the plots of New Comedy, however, including that of *Epitrepontes*, will only work if this requirement is given a liberal interpretation. In *Epitrepontes* the baby was conceived out of wedlock but was born after his parents had (fortuitously) married each other; once his parentage is established, his legitimacy is never questioned, and it is clear that Charisios need no longer rebuke himself for being 'the father of a bastard child' (896). In *Georgos* and *Samia* a child is actually born out of wedlock, yet in *Samia* (the end of *Georgos* is lost) the hot temper of Nikeratos is in the end completely assuaged by the assurance that Moschion will marry his daughter. One scenario that is discussed hypothetically in *Epitrepontes* would take this principle even further. Onesimos is reflecting on Pamphile's situation, now that Charisios has been proved to be the father of (as everyone supposes) a baby not hers:

> My mistress's position is precarious. If a girl is found who's the daughter of a free man[16] and was the mother of this baby, then he'll quickly marry her and [divorce] this one [Pamphile].

Epitr. 566–70

In this imagined scenario, the baby would not only have been conceived out of wedlock, it would have been born while its father was married not to its mother but to a third party; and yet it is not to be supposed that the new bride's parents would accept bastard (and therefore non-citizen) status for their grandson.[17] In Menander's treatment of legal issues, however, especially about hypothetical situations like this, 'we must allow for the possibility both of minor errors and of indifference to detail[; t]he legal issues may even have been unclear to Menander and his audience themselves' (Brown 1983: 418).[18] At Athens, indeed, no legal issue was ever clear unless there was a law that made explicit and unambiguous provision for it, since jurors were bound only by the text of the law (and, if this failed them, their sense of justice), not by precedent nor by any authoritative interpretation. It is quite likely that nobody knew for sure whether in these convoluted circumstances a child would be legitimate or not. And if Charisios swore the required oath at the child's phratry induction,[19] then provided that no one raised an objection, the child's legitimacy and citizenship would probably in practice be secure.

But at the time of the baby's birth, Pamphile believed him to be the bastard child of an unknown father, and she arranged for him to be abandoned in the woods. Infant exposure was a recognized phenomenon of Athenian life, though not one that was much talked about in public;[20] a child might be thus disposed of not only because it was illegitimate[21] but because it had a serious birth defect, or because its parents already had as many children as they could afford to rear,[22] or merely because it was a girl.[23] If the exposed baby died of starvation and/or hypothermia, no guilt, legal or even ritual, attached to the person who exposed it. Alternatively it might be picked up, most likely to be kept or sold as a slave.[24] Myth, and tragedy (see Chapter 8), often told of exposed babies who were afterwards reunited with their natal families; this was sometimes a blessing (as in the case of several pairs of twins who rescued their persecuted mothers: see p. 107 n. 25) and sometimes a curse (as in the cases of Oedipus and Paris). In New Comedy reunion is the almost invariable outcome, and it is almost invariably[25] a blessing, presenting a family with an heir when it would otherwise have had none, a young man or woman with citizenship when his/her status had previously been low or obscure, and/or a couple with a marriage which would otherwise have been impossible. Often, as in *Epitrepontes*, the discovery of the child's parentage is facilitated by the identification of objects ('recognition-tokens', *gnōrismata*) which were left with him/her at the time of abandonment (in *Epitrepontes* the ring which Pamphile had seized from her assailant).

All these three institutions are in New Comedy closely related to a fourth, that of marriage. By Menander's time it was a fundamental principle of Athenian society that a citizen could be validly married only to another citizen. This had become a *de facto* rule with the passage of Pericles' law of 451/0 restricting citizenship to the children of two citizen parents, and at a later date it was explicitly enshrined in law ([Demosthenes] 59.16–17). But this was not the only requirement for a valid marriage. There was no way for a couple to become lawfully man and wife unless the bride was either 'adjudged' to the bridegroom by the *archon* or by a court,[26] or (much more often) 'given in trust' (*enguētē*) to him by her *kyrios*, normally her father, 'for the procreation of legitimate children' as the regular betrothal formula had it (e.g. *Samia* 727). If at all possible, the *kyrios* also gave his son-in-law a dowry (*proix*); the dowries of New Comedy tend to be unrealistically large, but even by New Comic standards the four-talent dowry given by Smikrines to Charisios is right at the top of the scale.[27]

The dowry served as an incentive to marry (and especially to marry into a rich family), but it also had what may be called an insurance function. When a marriage ended, for whatever reason (other than death),[28] the dowry had to be repaid, and this potential sanction had a significant impact on the *de facto* power relations between husband and wife, particularly if the dowry was large in relation to the husband's own resources. Smikrines may express his indignation in a comically exaggerated way, but many another father-in-law would understand the implied argument:

He's been given a dowry of four talents, and yet he hasn't regarded himself as his wife's servant.

Epitr. 134–5

A marriage could be dissolved[29] not only on the initiative of the husband or the wife, but also on that of the wife's original *kyrios*.[30] For a divorce by the husband no formality at all was required: he simply dismissed his wife from his home (but then, as we have seen, he also had to return her dowry). The wife could not expel her husband from the marital home (for it was *he* who owned or rented it), but she could leave it herself; this, however, did not effect a divorce until it was registered with the *archon*,[31] and in any case the wife would need to have the protection of her natal family (to whom her dowry would revert) to assure both her maintenance and, if possible, her remarriage.

Most surprising to the modern mind, and most crucial in *Epitrepontes*, is the right of the wife's original *kyrios* to terminate her marriage. Both in *Epitrepontes* and in another, unidentified play in which this right is exercised[32] the wife protests strongly at this treatment, but in both cases it is clear that she has no right to veto it. Smikrines does in the end, though, go away without his daughter, perhaps because she has shown herself so determined not to leave voluntarily that her father realizes he would have to physically drag her away, for which he is neither sufficiently strong nor sufficiently tyrannical.[33] When he eventually returns, he discovers that she and Charisios are firmly united again and the parents of a son; this may have extinguished his legal right to end the marriage, and it certainly seems to have extinguished his desire to do so.

A young citizen woman in New Comedy need not be a virgin on marriage, but any previous sexual experience must be either (a) *involuntary* (as in the case of Pamphile) or (b) *in a stable relationship* formed at a time when she was not aware of, or could not prove, her citizen status (as in the case of Glykera in *Perikeiromene*), and must in any case be *with the man who subsequently becomes her husband* and no other. Women whose behaviour does not obey this rule are almost always sex-workers; the neutral term for these is *hetairai* ('female companions'), but they may be disparagingly labelled *pornai* ('whores'), as Habrotonon is by Smikrines at *Epitr.* 646 and 794. Some, like Habrotonon, are slaves owned by a *pornoboskos* ('whoremaster') and hired out to clients, either for their exclusive use (as Habrotonon is hired by Charisios for twelve drachmae a day) or as part of the equipment of a symposium; some are free women who can make their own terms for an exclusive relationship of specified or indefinite duration – though with no security comparable to the married woman's dowry, they are liable to instant dismissal with nothing but the clothes they stand up in.[34] Even a stable relationship between a *hetaira* and a young bachelor, like the one probably established at the end of *Epitrepontes* between Chairestratos and Habrotonon, was bound to end after a few years when the man wished to marry, though there was some degree of expectation that he would give his mistress a good pay-off to help her re-establish an independent life.[35]

Sexual relations between a married man and a *hetaira* were not in themselves considered a grievous wrong against his wife, though they might become so if he brought a mistress into the marital home, or spent resources on her that were needed for the maintenance of his wife and children, or otherwise made it evident that the *hetaira* took first place in his affections. Charisios' actions and inactions towards Habrotonon repeatedly show his ideas and emotions in conflict. First he hires her, at very considerable expense[36] and presumably not because of her musical skills, and yet for three days he does not touch her;[37] evidently he feels that to become her lover would be to repudiate his wife, and that this he cannot do. Then Habrotonon comes to him carrying a baby, a ring, and an entirely plausible tale of a rape committed on an occasion when Charisios knows he did in fact commit a rape – and the ethical calculations change, for he now has the interests of his son to consider. To save the boy from being reared as a slave (cf. 468–70, 539–40) he must buy Habrotonon and set her free, and since she will be bringing up his child, he will need to make some provision towards her maintenance – and Smikrines is quite correct in pointing out that this is bound to be at Pamphile's expense. Next Pamphile's defiance of her father heaps coals of fire on Charisios' head, and in his determination to reward her loyalty with his own he seems to forget about Habrotonon completely. This will not, however, worry the audience, who already know that the baby is not Habrotonon's but Pamphile's – and know, too, that Pamphile herself now knows this. Charisios has in fact no duties towards Habrotonon, and his duties to his son and his wife are not in conflict; but before becoming aware of that, he has done a far greater service for Habrotonon than he would have done by succumbing to her charms.

Characters

There are nine speaking characters in *Epitrepontes* (not counting the god who is generally thought to have appeared to deliver a delayed prologue), and three non-speaking characters with significant roles, namely Syriskos' wife, Sophrone, and the baby. All the speaking characters are carefully, consistently and distinctively drawn, as also (her silence notwithstanding) is Sophrone, and the personality of each of them (again including Sophrone)[1] makes an essential contribution to the happy outcome.[2] They will be examined here in the order of their appearance in the play.

Onesimos and **Karion**, who open the play, have two important characteristics in common. As Karion observes early on (F 2), they are both 'busybodies' (*periergoi*) who like to know as much as possible about other people's business; both of them, too, but especially Onesimos, are inclined to be loose-tongued. Onesimos displayed both these qualities shortly after the birth and exposure of Pamphile's baby, when he discovered what had happened[3] and then told Charisios about it, thus causing Charisios' decision to leave home – a decision which threatened to destroy his marriage and yet ultimately saved it by bringing him into contact with Habrotonon. Within the play itself, his curiosity leads him to listen in to Syriskos inventorying the objects found with the baby and recently surrendered by Daos, and thus to recognize Syriskos' description of the ring (387–90) as that of one which his master had lost. He feels impelled to claim the ring by a sense of duty to his master (at 395 he calls the ring 'ours'), but as is typical of comic slaves, his prime loyalty is to himself, and for fear of the possible consequences to himself he might never have revealed his discovery of the ring (cf. 419–29) had he not been persuaded by Habrotonon that for the baby's sake and his own[4] the truth must be ascertained (468–70).

Comic cooks[5] tend to be inordinately proud of their profession (which was generally regarded as rather a humble one) and inordinately inclined to talk about it. Karion may have conformed to this stereotype to some extent: a rather obscure passage by the rhetorician Themistius (*Basanistes* 262c; fourth century AD) seems to speak of his talking in an irritating manner about sauces. From the surviving text, in which hardly a complete sentence of his has been preserved, it is hard to judge. However, when Chairestratos' lunch party breaks up in Act III (603–29 approximately), it is Karion's loquacity[6] that reveals to Smikrines (whose presence Karion apparently for some time does not notice) that Charisios is believed to be the father of a child by Habrotonon, and thus triggers Smikrines' decision, crucial to the plot, to take Pamphile away from her husband.

Chairestratos, who is next to appear, is notable chiefly for his loyalty to his friend Charisios, whom he took in as a resident guest when Charisios felt he needed to leave home. When it first becomes evident that Smikrines is on the warpath against Charisios, he quickly agrees with Habrotonon that Charisios must be warned (165). Towards the end of Act III he tries to defend Charisios against Smikrines' fierce invectives – not very effectively, though it is doubtful whether anyone could have done better against Smikrines in this mood – and then goes off to fulfil a task, commissioned by Charisios, whose successful completion, he knows, will be very bad news for himself (699–701), and returns telling himself he must now forget about Habrotonon 'if you are to remain a faithful friend to Charisios, as you were before' (983–4). It is a little harder to find a specific contribution of his to the outcome of the story than it is for most other characters, but one wonders if it was he who suggested hiring Habrotonon to comfort Charisios with her music and in other ways. Charisios – who is still in love with Pamphile, and will take no interest whatever in Habrotonon – would hardly, one feels, have taken such an initiative himself, though once the suggestion was made he went along with it and offered to pay the high price demanded. If the play ends with Chairestratos firmly coupled with Habrotonon, and inviting both Charisios and Smikrines to a reconciliation party, both his behaviour and his reward are appropriate.

Smikrines, the only old man in the play, is both its strongest and (with the possible exception of Daos) its least sympathetic character. His ruling characteristic is the paramountcy in his mind of his personal, material interests. He is not to be condemned merely for wanting to end his daughter's marriage, when her husband had deserted her and was seemingly on the point of setting up house with a *hetaira*; but his complete disregard of her own arguments and wishes, and the emphasis he obsessively lays on the squandering, and later on the return, of her dowry and on other monetary questions (127–39, 687–8, 749–50, 1065–7), indicate that he sees the whole matter primarily in a financial light. Yet in the arbitration scene, where his own material interests are seemingly not involved, his scale of values is quite different, and he rightly awards the baby, and everything found with it, to Syriskos who is clearly seeking what is best for the child, and not to Daos who would be content for the child to grow up a slave rather than that he should lose a few drachmas' worth of jewellery. This decision, of course, brings the baby, and its trinkets including the all-important ring, into the vicinity of Chairestratos' house, where Onesimos sees them. Later, Smikrines' decision to end his daughter's marriage will rouse her to the defiance that moves her listening husband so deeply.

Habrotonon[7] is a *hetaira*, but not of the common mercenary type, in part no doubt because, being a slave, she cannot keep the money she earns.[8] Altruism shines through almost everything she does. It is she who first suggests warning Charisios of the arrival of Smikrines (164). From the moment she sees the baby, she loves it, and with remarkable cleverness contrives a scheme that will with luck determine – as it does – whether Charisios is indeed the child's father;[9] as Onesimos points out, her ruse is also likely to win her her freedom, but that is a bonus rather than an initial motive. She carries out the plan brilliantly, and one consequence of this is that she is in possession of the baby when she happens to come face to face with Pamphile. Her spontaneous joy on finding the baby's mother, and her pleasure in telling Charisios – 'sweetheart' (*glukutate*) she calls him[10] – that the child whom he thought to be hers is actually his wife's, make it understandable that many male scholars have developed a soft spot for Habrotonon and feel some regret that her reward can be no more than freedom plus an agreeable, but inevitably temporary, relationship with Chairestratos.[11]

Daos appears only in the arbitration scene. His most prominent characteristic is selfishness, evidenced by his attempt to retain the objects found with the baby; he resembles Smikrines in having an unhealthy obsession with material wealth. But like Smikrines, he is not a total villain – and it is his better side that is crucial in moving the action of the play towards its goal. He it was that first found the baby, and he took it home intending to bring it up himself (245–51; apparently, unlike Syriskos, he lives alone). He does not explain why he did this. It cannot have been solely or even primarily the value of the trinkets, otherwise he could simply have taken them and left the baby where it was; rather, he must have pitied the child. And when he began to have second thoughts because of the trouble and expense involved in child-rearing (252–5), he did not re-expose the baby but handed him over to Syriskos – though one doubts whether it really took Syriskos 'the whole day' (270) to persuade him to do so. These are the two actions by Daos that contribute to the outcome of the action; thereafter he becomes a menace to it.

Syriskos has, for a slave, considerable intellectual pretensions. His eloquence and rhetorical skills (and his knowledge of myth and tragedy, 320–37) carry the day in the arbitration hearing. Afterwards he carefully inventories the articles that had been left with the baby, giving a detailed description of each that is worthy of an auctioneer's catalogue (382–404), overheard by Onesimos who recognizes the description of the ring. Throughout his time on stage in Act II he is accompanied by his wife; she had recently lost her own baby (268), and one may well suppose that in begging Daos to give him the foundling, Syriskos was thinking of her happiness at least as much as of his own. When Syriskos goes off to town (462–3) his wife remains in Chairestratos' house and looks after the baby (464–5) until Habrotonon takes him over.

The partners to the troubled marriage, **Pamphile** and **Charisios**, come on stage separately (they never appear together) for the first time in Act IV. Pamphile is splendidly defiant of her father, and utterly devoted to a husband who has thus far done absolutely nothing to deserve her devotion. One might be reminded of a tragic character like the Euripidean Andromache, who as the wife of Hector had tolerated all his extramarital affairs and even suckled his bastard children (*Andromache* 222–5), while as the concubine of Neoptolemus she tolerated his marriage to Hermione of Sparta until Hermione began plotting to murder her. One must, however, bear in mind, first that the prospect of going back to live with a father like Smikrines, followed by a probable remarriage to the kind of man he would find congenial, is hardly an inviting one, and secondly that Pamphile knows, as Smikrines does not, that she committed a serious wrong against Charisios by concealing the fact that when she married him she was pregnant, as she believed, by another man. When an angry Smikrines goes off to fetch Sophrone for a final assault on Pamphile, Pamphile is at perhaps the lowest point in her life, estranged from father and husband alike and expecting never to see her son again – when in fact she will see him in a minute or two. That meeting with her baby, and with Habrotonon who knows who its father was, was made possible by Pamphile's argument with her father: but for that, she would either have been indoors when Habrotonon came outside, or else well on the way back to her father's house.

Although Charisios is the person on whom the thoughts of others have mostly been focused since the beginning of the play, he has made almost the smallest positive contribution to the restoration of his own happiness at the end of it. What has he done? He has committed a rape, the product of so impersonal a lust that he did not at the time know who his victim was. He has got married, to a rich man's daughter who brought with her an exceptionally large dowry. Not long afterwards he went away, perhaps for two or three months, on a business trip. On his return, shocked by the news that Pamphile had given birth, he left home again and tried to obliterate his sorrows with a heavy dose of pleasure, including the hiring of Habrotonon (which may, as suggested above, have been done at Chairestratos' suggestion, but for which Charisios paid). Confronted by Habrotonon, and presented with his own ring, he admits to being the father of the baby in Habrotonon's arms; this 'discovery' leads him to send Chairestratos to town to buy Habrotonon's freedom – almost the first constructive action of his that we have heard of. He then overhears much of the quarrel between Pamphile and her father, is amazed by her loyalty and love, feels a new and shaming awareness of his own shortcomings,[12] and resolves to stand by her and present a united front to Smikrines.[13] Immediately afterwards he is told the happy truth, to whose revelation he has hardly contributed at all except by the fortunate chance that the music-girl whom his money brought to Chairestratos' house had been present on the night of the rape and had seen the victim. And yet we must remember that he has throughout been unable to repudiate his love for Pamphile. He could have divorced her, and he might have had a good moral case for retaining the dowry on the ground that the marriage had been made under false pretences (he would surely never have married her had he known she was already pregnant); but instead of dismissing her from his home, he withdrew from it himself leaving her in possession of it. He could have started an affair with Habrotonon, for whose services he was paying a high price and who both expected and wished to have him as a lover (432); in fact he took virtually no notice of her until she tricked him into believing that she was the mother of his child. Others helped bring about the dénouement by what they did or said: Charisios helped bring it about by what he did not do.

The last character to appear, Pamphile's old nurse **Sophrone**,[14] does not speak on stage, though (as 1062–75 shows) she is to be imagined as having said a great deal to Smikrines, most of it not at all to his liking, shortly before coming on stage. It had no effect on Smikrines except to annoy him; nor does anything else in this part of Act V until he begins to realize (1131–3) that he has a legitimate grandson. Sophrone, however, clearly knew all about the exposure of Pamphile's baby (cf. 1117–29) and had probably herself been involved in arranging it.

Thus the outcome of the action has been crucially dependent on the virtues, and sometimes also the vices, of almost all the characters. We may start from the point at which Pamphile, having given birth five months after her marriage, bowed to the inevitable and had her baby exposed. Had not Onesimos' busybodiness led him to discover the truth about the birth and exposure; or had not his talkativeness led him to reveal it to his master; or had not Charisios' continuing love of his wife inhibited him from divorcing her; or had not Chairestratos' friendship caused him to take Charisios in as a guest and (perhaps) to persuade him to hire Habrotonon; or had not Daos' pity led him to take up the abandoned baby; or had not his profit-and-loss mentality led him to hand it over to Syriskos; or had not his talkativeness led him to reveal to another shepherd (who then told Syriskos) that some trinkets had been left with the baby (299–301); or had Syriskos been less eloquent than he was, or Smikrines less capable of seeing where justice lay in a case apparently not affecting his own interests; or had Syriskos' intellectual pretensions not led him to give a connoisseur's description of the ring that had belonged to Charisios; or had not Onesimos' busybodiness (again) led him to eavesdrop on Syriskos; or had his sense of duty to his master not led him to demand the handing over of what he called 'our' ring; or had not Habrotonon's ingenuity, together with her fondness for the baby, given her the inspired idea of pretending to be its mother; or had she not implemented that idea so brilliantly; or had not Karion's typically cook-like annoyance at losing his fee led him to vent his dissatisfaction out of doors, in the presence of Smikrines; or had not Smikrines' own profit-and-loss mentality made him resolve to break up his daughter's marriage; or had not Pamphile's loyalty to her husband made her resist her father's will – then the son of Charisios and Pamphile would never have been reunited with his parents (or at any rate not with *both* of them), and would have grown up as a slave or, at best, as a bastard without the citizen rights to which his actual birth, to parents who at the time were married, should have entitled him. It thus took at least seventeen actions or omissions by nine different characters, as well as some strokes of pure luck (notably the coincidences of Habrotonon's presence both at the beginning and at the end of the whole story, and of the arranged marriage of Pamphile to the same man who had raped her some months before), to produce the outcome; and if any of the nine personalities had been different in relevant respects, that outcome could not have happened.[15]

Of the key character traits, some are virtues and some are vices. Vices that appear more than once are a loose tongue (in slaves and cooks), excessive inquisitiveness (in Onesimos), and what I have called the profit-and-loss mentality shared by the richest person in the story (Smikrines) and the poorest (Daos). Of the virtues, by far the most prominent is loyalty – to spouse, to friends, to master or mistress – which is displayed conspicuously, though in different degrees, by (in alphabetical order) Chairestratos, Charisios, Onesimos, Pamphile and also Sophrone; that of Pamphile, in particular, as we have seen, is in the circumstances altogether extraordinary. Next after this comes the instinctive fondness and protectiveness that most people feel towards small children, which has some impact even on a man like Daos, is evidently powerful with Syriskos, is exploited by him to influence Smikrines, and is an important motive for Habrotonon even though she has no particular desire to be a mother herself (547). It will be seen that every significant character except the cook Karion is shown to possess one or the other of these two virtues, and that of the two great confrontations in the play, the arbitration scene in Act II and the argument between Smikrines and Pamphile in Act IV, the first sees the victory of the child-nurturing instinct and the second that of marital loyalty (in Pamphile during the confrontation itself, in Charisios in its aftermath).

Structural Patterns

The action of *Epitrepontes*, particularly when considered in conjunction with its back-story, can be seen to be elaborately structured in multiple ways. This chapter will explore some of the most important of these patterns.

The baby's journey. In one of its aspects *Epitrepontes*, like several of Menander's other plays, is about the establishment of the true parentage (in effect, the true identity) of a child. When the child is in earliest infancy, it is always male and is always recognized in the end as the legitimate son and heir of a young male citizen of good family, who either marries the baby's mother towards the end of the play or else (as in *Epitrepontes*) by a providential coincidence has married her already. Once so recognized, the baby will of course become, if it is not already, a resident in its father's house. In *Epitrepontes* the baby was actually born in that house; but it then has a long and hazardous journey, passing through several pairs of hands, before it eventually comes back to stay.

If, as is likely, he was represented on stage by a suitably dressed doll, the baby was by far the most important of the 'props' in the production of *Epitrepontes* – and almost all the play's other known significant 'props' (see list in Tordoff 2013: 107) are belongings of his, being objects that were left with him when he was exposed in the woods. He himself, though a 'mute' character, is present on stage for a total of about 230 lines in Acts II and IV – more than either his mother (about 180, all in Act IV) or his father (about 140 in Acts IV and V) or, indeed, any of the adults who have charge of him (see below on 'custodians' nos. 1–8) with the possible exception of Habrotonon.

The baby was brought into the world by *Pamphile* (custodian number one), who believed him to be a bastard, conceived as the result of a rape by an unknown man. She acted in the manner that society tacitly condoned, by having the baby exposed, probably through the agency of *Sophrone* (custodian number two); but she left with it a few pieces of jewellery, partly as a sort of endowment to help anyone who took up the child to support it, and partly in the hope that one item (the ring seized from the rapist) might eventually help to identify the father.

The baby was left in the woods, and it cannot have lain there very long before it was picked up by *Daos* (custodian number three). His motives may have been mixed, and if he had kept the baby he might not have proved a very good father; but his action may nevertheless have saved the baby's life. Next day he met *Syriskos* (custodian number four) and on his earnest request gave him the baby (but not the jewellery). This for the first time provided the baby with a foster mother as well as a foster father, as he was looked after, and presumably breastfed, by *Syriskos' wife* (custodian number five), who is holding the child at the beginning of the arbitration scene when it first appears on stage. Up to this point, from the time of its abandonment, the baby had been in male hands; now it is returned to the care of women.

As Syriskos is a slave belonging to Chairestratos, and has business with his master, his wife brings the baby into Chairestratos' house, and thus into proximity with its actual father, Charisios. There it is taken over by *Habrotonon* (custodian number six) as part of her pretence that she is its mother; she is the fourth slave in succession to have charge of the child,[1] and she apparently keeps him until she meets *Pamphile* (custodian number seven). It is not clear whether she gives Pamphile the baby before the pair go into Charisios' house at 877, but at any rate the child is now back where he belongs, though his father is not yet aware of the fact. When he is made aware, the baby who started as Pamphile's bastard, and then was cared for by slave after slave after slave, has become the legitimate son of *Pamphile and Charisios* (joint custodians number eight).

Smikrines: 'his dowry and his daughter'.[2] All through the play Smikrines is campaigning to impose his will on his daughter, or his son-in-law, or both, with the prime objective of safeguarding or recovering his dowry, and in this campaign he gets absolutely nowhere. His first attempt, in Act I, is tentative: he interacts with Chairestratos only briefly if at all, and then goes in to see how things are with his daughter,[3] intending then to 'consider how to tackle that man [Charisios]'. We do not know what passed between him and Pamphile, but whatever she may have said, it will have made little difference to him, and he would no doubt have walked straight into Chairestratos' house to confront Charisios had not Onesimos sent him on a wild-goose chase to the city. He is destined never to enter Chairestratos' house, and never to meet Charisios, until the very end of the play when Chairestratos probably invited both him and his son-in-law to a reconciliation party.

Smikrines' departure for the city is delayed by the arbitration episode (to which we will return), and while there he discovers that Charisios' behaviour has become the talk of the town, and his anger, inflamed by this public scandal (which impinges on his own reputation, since it casts him as a man who has given his daughter to a neglectful, loose-living wastrel), is then heightened yet further by learning that Charisios has fathered a child by Habrotonon. He rants and raves at the innocent Chairestratos, and decides to remove Pamphile, and end the marriage, forthwith.[4] The whole sequence is a repetition of Smikrines' intervention in Act I, but a repetition at a much higher intensity; and Act III ends, as Act I did, with Smikrines entering Charisios' house to talk to Pamphile – but this time with the fixed intention of taking her away with him.

His first assault was frustrated by deception. His second is frustrated by direct defiance. Despite initial protestations of respect for her father (799–805), Pamphile speaks as if her sole duty now was to her husband, regardless of his behaviour. Smikrines can thus remove her only by force, and to do that would create further scandal against him. He apparently decides instead to make another attempt at persuasion in a third visit to Pamphile, this time with the help of Sophrone.

But before he returns, we are treated to an imaginary confrontation between him and Charisios, whose feelings have been transformed by witnessing Pamphile's insistence on standing by her man. When Smikrines comes back for Pamphile, he will find Charisios at home, and Charisios will send him away with a flea in his ear:

Her father will treat her very roughly. But what do I care about him? I'll say straight out, 'Stop bothering me, Smikrines. My wife's not leaving me. So why are you harassing and coercing Pamphile?'

927

Few commentators have believed that, had that scenario materialized, Charisios would really have had the courage to speak to Smikrines in those terms, even after learning, as he soon does, that the mother of his baby is not Habrotonon but Pamphile herself. But it never happens anyway. The first time he came, Smikrines was defeated by a slave; the second time, by a woman, and his own daughter at that; and this third time he will be defeated by a male slave and a female ex-slave.

Sophrone is clearly going to be of no assistance to Smikrines at all, despite his threats of violence and even murder (1073); she disapproves of what he is doing and has said so (though not on stage, where she remains entirely silent). When Onesimos comes to the door, he immediately begins to make fun of Smikrines, calling him a robber (1082), giving him a theological-ethical lecture (1084–1100) and then a finger-wagging warning:

Don't let me catch you being rash again, I warn you. And now forget about your grievances and come in and give a hug and a greeting to your grandson.

1110–13

All told, Onesimos toys with Smikrines for some seventy lines, and when a third person appears it is not Charisios but Chairestratos, apparently with further rebukes for the old man (sweet revenge, after the way Smikrines had treated him in Act III). It is possible that Smikrines was then again sent away, as his namesake is in *Aspis*; but this would be an unsatisfactory conclusion. Smikrines in *Aspis* was an unmitigated villain,[5] and was childless. Smikrines in *Epitrepontes* has a better self, which we have already seen displayed; he also has a daughter, and while he never forgets about her dowry, the arguments with which he tried to persuade her to leave her husband were directed mainly to her welfare and were quite cogent. It would not be satisfactory to end the play with the quarrel between Pamphile's husband and her father still unresolved. Rather it should end with a feast involving all the three free male characters, and the appearance of Chairestratos suggests that he will be the host, so that Smikrines, who had hovered outside his house during much of the first three acts, is at last able to enter it.

We had known since Act II that he was capable of better things, when not blinded by self-interest; and indeed one may say that he is divinely rewarded for his just decision. For though he does not know it, he has decided the fate of his own grandson, and his decision gives an outcome which is best for the little boy and will eventually prove to be best for Smikrines too. It earns him compliments and blessings from the honest Syriskos (358, 370–1), though Daos never stops grumbling.

Even to Syriskos, however, Smikrines has spoken roughly in the earlier part of the scene (especially 228–30, 248–9). In fact there is not a single character in the play to whom, or about whom, Smikrines has not spoken in harsh terms, except possibly for his daughter[6] and the cook Karion. And he is singularly ineffective in exercising influence on others: as the case of Sophrone shows, he cannot control even his own (ex-)slaves.

The two (or three) houses. In *Epitrepontes*, as in most Menandrian plays, the action unfolds in front of (and to some extent, unseen, inside) two houses, in this case those of Charisios and Chairestratos. In some plays there is also a third important interior space with an entrance visible to the audience, such as the sanctuary of Pan and the Nymphs in *Dyskolos*. In *Epitrepontes* too there is a third important interior space, but it is at a distance and not part of the stage setting: the house of Smikrines, which Pamphile left a few months ago on her marriage to Charisios and to which her father now wants her to return. He fails, and he remains the only free-born person to enter that house.

Charisios' house is also, for most of the play, under-occupied. Until the second half of Act IV its only resident (that we hear of) is Pamphile,[7] its only visitor Smikrines. The first other person to join Pamphile in this house is, surprisingly, Habrotonon, and at the same time the baby returns to the home which he has never seen since the day of his birth.

Charisios joins his wife once he has been told the truth about the baby (Habrotonon meanwhile returning to Chairestratos' house),[8] and Onesimos will soon have followed him; so the house which during most of Act IV (at the start of which Smikrines and Pamphile come outside) had no dramatically relevant persons in it at all now shelters four people, including one complete nuclear family who at the start of the play were widely scattered – Pamphile in the marital home, Charisios next door in Chairestratos' house, and the baby presumably in the unpretentious charcoal-burner's hut, in or near the woods, where Syriskos and his wife lived.

But most of the play's activity takes place in and around Chairestratos' house. It begins with a party in progress there, and it probably ended with preparations for another, once again with Charisios as a principal guest and Habrotonon also present. But how different the two parties are in every other respect! The first (one of three held on successive days (440–1) – or four at least, if we assume that there were evening symposia as well as daytime ones) was a bachelor affair with wine (and, to Smikrines' annoyance, money) flowing freely, Charisios a refugee from a marriage only a few months old which seems to have gone disastrously wrong, and Habrotonon a whoremaster's slave hired primarily to provide sexual services (for Charisios, or so she understands; but many of the others present apparently fancy her, and several of them – though not, it would seem, Chairestratos himself – try to press themselves upon her, 430–1). The party with which the play concluded will have been a celebration of the reintegration of two families, united by a restored marriage, and of the discovery of a true-born heir to both of them. The rowdy young men of the lunch party have gone, and in their place has come a hopefully mellowed Smikrines, now a happy grandfather (thanks partly to his own sense of justice in the arbitration episode).[9] Charisios is re-established in his home with the wife he has always desperately loved, and now with a son. Habrotonon is again the only female present, but she is no longer a slave nor a sex-worker available for hire; she is a free woman with the semi-respectable status of *pallake* to Chairestratos, and Smikrines, who called her a whore (fortunately not to her face, 794), now accepts her as a dining companion. Many of the intermediate events that paved the way for the dénouement also took place at Chairestratos' house. Outside it, Onesimos recognized his master's ring in the possession of Syriskos (who is Chairestratos' slave); inside it, Habrotonon carried out her plan to prove beyond doubt that Charisios was indeed the baby's father; at its door, Charisios listened and marvelled as his wife defied her father and refused to desert him even when he had already deserted her; through that same door, Habrotonon came shortly afterwards, carrying the baby on what proved to be the last lap of the odyssey we traced earlier in this chapter. Thus, paradoxically, the house that seemed to represent bachelor irresponsibility made a great contribution to the restoration of marital and family unity in the house next door.

The absent protagonist. From the start of the play – from the very first sentence, of which he is the subject – the thoughts, words and actions of most of the characters are centred on Charisios. In Act I, he seems to be the topic of most of the poorly preserved initial dialogue between Onesimos and Karion; the key piece of information given in the divine prologue must have been that Charisios was the father of Pamphile's baby; then we hear Smikrines grumbling about Charisios' extravagance, and Chairestratos and Habrotonon agreeing that he must be warned. In Act II, both Smikrines and the audience are for a long time distracted by the arbitration episode; but before that episode Onesimos was trying to protect Charisios by sending Smikrines off to the city in search of him, and after it his recognition of Charisios' ring starts a movement that will continue to Habrotonon's deception of Charisios and its consequences, which include further denunciations of Charisios by Smikrines and also probably Charisios' decision to purchase Habrotonon and set her free. In the opening scene of Act IV, Smikrines expatiates on what life will be like for Pamphile if she remains married to Charisios, and Pamphile insists that she *will* remain married to him come what may. She then learns, by meeting Habrotonon, that the mysterious baby is hers and that Charisios is its father. Then Onesimos recounts Charisios' extraordinary reaction to Pamphile's loyalty to him. And all this time – at least three-quarters of the play – Charisios himself, arguably its central character, has not appeared on stage at all. He enters for the first time at 908, and is present for the last 70 lines or so of Act IV; we saw in Chapter 4 that he was probably on stage for most of the first scene of Act V (when he may have made over Habrotonon to Chairestratos), and he may also have appeared briefly in the final scene of all.

The phenomenon of a central character who only comes on stage at a late point in a play is one that was not unknown in tragedy. Indeed, there was a whole subgenre, now often called *nostos* plays (plays of 'return'), of which this is almost a constitutive element. A prime example is the oldest tragedy we possess, Aeschylus' *Persians*. Its central character is undoubtedly Xerxes, who is presented as bearing an overwhelming responsibility for the disastrous invasion of Greece which has 'heaped Hades with Persians' (924); but Xerxes does not arrive until the play is more than five-sixths over,[10] so late that he has no spoken words to utter, only anapaestic chant (908–16) and lyric song thereafter. Other, less drastic instances include Aeschylus' *Agamemnon* and Euripides' *Madness of Heracles*, but the most extreme surviving specimen is Euripides' *Andromache*. In *Andromache* everything that happens, including the mortal peril in which Andromache and her son are placed, is traceable to the actions of Neoptolemus, in particular to his decision to marry Hermione (when she had previously been promised to Orestes, and when his captive Andromache had already given him a son) and his attempt to demand recompense from Apollo at Delphi for the death of his father Achilles; Neoptolemus, moreover, is the only significant person who dies during the play, and its last scene is one of mourning over his body.[11] And yet the living Neoptolemus does not appear at all in *Andromache*: he has left for Delphi before the action begins.

Menander's *Aspis* is a *nostos* play of a kind: Kleostratos has been away campaigning as a mercenary in Lycia, and returns home only towards the end of Act IV (at about the same point, that is, at which Charisios first comes on stage). However, Kleostratos has been reported dead, and most of the first three and a half acts are concerned with the question who is to marry his sister (now an *epikleros* or heiress, required to marry the nearest relative who puts in a claim) and thereby gain possession of his estate (consisting mainly of war booty, which a faithful slave has brought home).

All these characters are in, or are returning from, distant parts. Charisios, by contrast, is only just offstage the whole time. The audience must be constantly expecting to see him, and as this expectation is repeatedly frustrated, they may begin to wonder whether they ever will, particularly when Charisios' reaction to Pamphile's defiance is reported by Onesimos instead of our hearing it from his own lips. It is thus a neat *coup de théâtre* to bring Charisios on for the first time directly after that report.[12]

Another character of whom a modern audience would expect to see more is Pamphile. The ancient audience, contrariwise, might have been surprised to see as much of her as they do (it seems certain that her one period on stage, 702–877, is longer than Charisios' two or three spells combined). A young wife (and Pamphile, married only a few months, can hardly be more than sixteen), like an unmarried maiden, was expected to stay out of the public eye – as indeed Pamphile would have done, had her father not been so determined to take her home with him. For all her outpourings of emotion (at the time of the rape, probably at the time the baby was exposed, and thirdly when she thinks she is about to lose her husband as well as her child) she gives the impression of being more effectively assertive than Charisios, and one might well feel that of the two she would be the better person to have at one's side in any dispute that was not likely to end in physical violence.

Literary and Intellectual Background

It was recognized in antiquity that in important respects Menandrian comedy was almost as much the descendant of the tragic drama of Sophocles and, especially, Euripides as it was of the comic drama of Aristophanes and his contemporaries. As the Roman critic Quintilian put it (*Institutio Oratoria* 10.1.69):

> Menander both admired Euripides greatly, as he often testifies, and followed in his footsteps, even though working in a different genre.

The reunion of long-separated parents and children, or siblings, or husbands and wives, had been a favourite theme of Euripidean tragedy, represented among his surviving plays respectively by *Ion, Iphigeneia in Tauris*, and *Helen*, all of which are generally thought to have been produced within a couple of years of each other in 414–12 bc; another play of the same period, *Andromeda*, is one of the earliest known tragedies[1] in which love, leading to marriage, was the strongest factor driving the plot. In the fourth century Euripides became the most popular of the classical tragedians, and according to Aristotle (*Poetics* 1453a30-36) plots like those of *Iphigeneia in Tauris* and *Helen* were particularly favoured:

> The second-best [kind of tragic plot] is the structure which some rank first, where the play has a double structure like that of the *Odyssey*, with different final outcomes for the better and worse characters.[2] It is held to rank first because of theatre audiences' lack of fibre, since the poets follow the wishes and preferences of their public; but this is not the kind of pleasure that properly belongs to tragedy, being more at home in comedy.

Here Aristotle is thinking primarily of the myth-based comedies that were common fare when he first came to Athens, for he illustrates his point by saying that 'those who are the greatest of enemies in myth, like Orestes and Aegisthus, have become friends by the time of their final exit' (1453a36-38); but the principle applies equally to the freely invented comic plots which had become the norm by Menander's time and which he himself invariably uses. And in the creation of these plots he often finds a measure of inspiration in Euripides (more rarely in Sophocles).[3]

Twice in the surviving portions of *Epitrepontes* explicit reference is made to tragic parallels. In the arbitration scene (325–43) Syriskos is arguing that the objects exposed with the baby may one day serve as crucial evidence of his identity and kindred:

> You've seen the tragedies, I know, and you're aware of all this. That Neleus and Pelias were found by an old goatherd, wearing a leather jerkin just like mine, but when he realized that they were his superiors he told the story of how he had found them and picked them up, and he gave them each a little pouch of identification tokens, from which they learned all about themselves and from goatherds they became kings . . . By means of recognition tokens a man has avoided marrying his sister, another met and rescued his mother, a third saved his brother.[4]

And almost at the end of the play another slave, Onesimos, also addressing Smikrines and revealing with exquisite slowness and obscurity the truth about Pamphile's baby, suggests a parallel with another Euripidean princess:

> "Twas Nature willed it, who cares naught for laws;
> For this was woman made.'
> Why are you so thick? If you don't eventually get it, Smikrines, I'll have
> to give you a complete tragic speech from *Augē*!
>
>   1133–6

The quotation (now Euripides fr. 265a) had been known before the discovery of the Cairo codex, but it had not been known which play it came from.

There are important parallels between *Auge* and *Epitrepontes*, as is evident from the account of the myth given by the fifth-century Armenian bishop Moses of Chorene (*Progymnasmata* 3.3):

When a festival of Athena was being celebrated in a certain town of Arcadia, and her priestess Auge, daughter of Aleos, was leading a chorus in a night-time ritual, she was raped by Heracles[5] who left her a ring as evidence of his crime and then quitted the region. She became pregnant with his child and gave birth to Telephus . . . When the rape became known to Auge's father, he flared up with rage and ordered Telephus to be cast away in a desert place (where he was suckled by a doe) and Auge to be drowned. At this juncture Heracles returned to the district, was informed of the result of his act by means of the ring, admitted paternity of the child and saved its mother from imminent death.

Pamphile too was raped at a night festival, was forced to have her child exposed (though forced by circumstances rather than by a cruel father), and used a ring left by the rapist[6] as a recognition token.

But Menander also enjoys exploiting the knowledge of tragedy that most of his audience will have possessed, *without* spelling out the connection. In *Samia*, for example, the basic constellation of characters corresponds closely to that of Euripides' two *Hippolytus* plays: a father (Theseus/Demeas) returns from abroad to find that his son (Hippolytus/ Moschion – respectively, a bastard son and an adopted son) has apparently violated his (the father's) wife or mistress (Phaedra/Chrysis). But while the characters of *Samia* refer to a considerable number of mythical or tragic precedents (Helen, Oedipus, Thyestes, Danaë . . .), they never make any mention of Hippolytus or Phaedra.

A similar challenge appears to be posed in *Epitrepontes*, specifically in the iconic arbitration scene, which is clearly modelled on a scene of Euripides' play *Alope*.[7] The story is thus told by the Latin mythographer Hyginus (*Fabulae* 187; second century AD?):

Alope, the beautiful daughter of Cercyon, was raped by Neptune [= Poseidon], and gave birth to a son whom, unknown to her father, she gave to her nurse to be exposed; when he had been exposed, a mare came and suckled him. A shepherd . . . saw the baby, picked him up and took him home; the baby was clad in a royal robe. Another shepherd asked to be given the baby, and he gave it, but without the robe. When

the other demanded to be given this token of the boy's nobility, he was
refused and a quarrel arose between the two, and they went to King
Cercyon and argued the matter before him. The man who had been
given the baby began to demand the robe; when it was brought,
Cercyon perceived that it had been cut from a garment of his daughter's,
and the frightened nurse told him that Alope was the baby's mother.
He sentenced Alope to death by starvation,[8] and had the baby cast out.
But it was again fed by the mare and again found and picked up by
shepherds, who realized that divine power was seeing to it that he was
reared, and so brought him up and gave him the name Hippothous.
[Cercyon was later killed by Theseus and his kingdom given to
Hippothous; Alope's body was transformed by Neptune into a spring.]

Up to 'began to demand the robe', the story of *Epitrepontes* is in all
essentials identical to this, if we focus our gaze first on Pamphile and
then on the baby. Smikrines, like Cercyon, is unwittingly in the position
of deciding the fate of his own grandson. But whereas Cercyon is the
first person to discover the baby's identity, during the arbitration process
itself, Smikrines remains in ignorance[9] and will eventually become the
last person to learn the truth. That moment, when it comes, will be
marked by an explicit reference to the other Euripidean play that has
contributed to the plot of this comedy, *Auge*; the connection to *Alope*,
on the other hand, is marked, so far as we can tell, by no reference and
no quotation.

Menander is said to have been a pupil of Theophrastus, the successor
of Aristotle as head of the Lyceum, and as we have seen he got into
trouble at one time because of his friendship with another Aristotelian
philosopher, Demetrius of Phalerum. Some of his plays do seem to
deploy specifically Aristotelian concepts or arguments, and *Epitrepontes*
is one of them.[10]

In the fifth book of his *Nicomachean Ethics*, Aristotle is at one point
engaged in defining and classifying rightful (*dikaion*) and wrongful
(*adikon*) actions, and he points out the importance of distinguishing
between actions that are voluntary, those that are involuntary, and those
that cannot sensibly be given either designation (such as ageing and

dying, 1135b2). Acts done involuntarily, for example under compulsion or in fear, if they can be called rightful or wrongful at all, are so only 'incidentally' (*kata sumbebēkos*) (1136b2-8). But even among voluntary acts a further distinction must be made:

> Of voluntary acts, we do some from prior decision (*proelomenoi*) and others without such decision – premeditated and unpremeditated acts respectively. Thus there are three kinds of harm in society. If it is inflicted in ignorance, it is an error (*hamartēma*), when one acts under a misapprehension of the identity of the victim, or of the naturè of the act, or of the instrument, or of the objective; e.g. [a man wounds another with a javelin] when he had not intended to hit anyone, or not that particular person, or not with that weapon, or not with that effect, but what happened was different from what he intended – say, he meant only to prick rather than to wound ... When the harm occurs contrary to reasonable expectation, it is a *misfortune* (*atukhēma*); when it is foreseeable but not due to evil intent, it is an *error* (for one is said to err when the cause [of harm] originates within oneself, and to be unfortunate when the cause is external); if it is done with knowledge but without premeditation, it is a *wrong* (*adikēma*), for example things done through anger or other inevitable or natural human emotions – for those who inflict harm ... in this way act wrongfully and commit wrongs, but this does not make them evil or wicked men, because the harm was not inflicted out of wickedness; but when he acts from prior decision he is evil and wicked.

> 1135b8-25

Despite the reference to 'three kinds of harm', we actually have here a *fourfold* classification of harmful acts, corresponding roughly to the criteria by which coroners, police, prosecutors, judges and juries classify acts causing death as misadventure, manslaughter,[11] and second- and first-degree murder.[12] Menander makes use of this classification in several plays (see Cinaglia 2014); in *Epitrepontes* it is deployed especially, though not exclusively, by Pamphile and Charisios.

In the arbitration scene, Daos and Syriskos trade accusations of deliberate wrongdoing (*adikia*); Smikrines declares decisively that the wrongdoer is Daos (356, 357), though Daos still thinks, and may say explicitly at 371, that *he* is the wronged party.

After this, attention soon becomes concentrated on the baby and how it came to be, and at 499 (cf. also 508) an *adik-* word is used for the first time (so far as we know) in connection with the rape at the Tauropolia: Habrotonon does not want to find the baby's mother until she knows the identity of 'the man who wronged her' (*ton adikounta*). This is the normal categorization of rape, which can be found alike on the lips of the former nurse of the victim's mother (*Georgos* 30) and of a slave of the perpetrator addressing his master (*Samia* 68).[13]

The three key verbal roots *adik-, hamart-* and *tukh-* all appear in the space of two lines (perhaps, indeed, within a single sentence) in Pamphile's speech to her father in Act IV (807–8) as partly revealed by the new Michigan papyrus. Unfortunately that papyrus is very fragmentary, and the restoration of the text is difficult and disputed. There is something about a woman 'having done nothing wrong' (using the perfect participle of the verb *adikein*), and in the next line a reference to other women who have 'erred' (*hamartousas*) and whom Pamphile does not want to discuss (*eômen* 'let's leave them aside'). The latter are probably *hetairai* like Habrotonon, about whom Smikrines has had a great deal to say, all of it disparaging. As to 'having done nothing wrong', it is possible that Pamphile is here asserting her own innocence; but her father can hardly have accused her of deliberate wrongdoing (as opposed to mere folly), and a very tempting alternative (Römer 2012a) is to take the sentence containing this phrase as a question and suppose that Pamphile is in effect saying that she is *not*, or not necessarily, altogether innocent. And this is indeed true, in a sense of which Smikrines is and remains wholly unaware: for Pamphile had allowed herself to be married to Charisios when she was four months pregnant by, she believed, another, unknown man – a deliberate and grave deception of her husband (and also of her father, whom she had caused to give her in marriage under false pretences). By implying (reasonably enough) that this was an *adikēma* but speaking of professional sex-workers only as *hamartousai*, Pamphile indicates that she thinks herself a worse delinquent than they. She must feel very guilty indeed, despite having been placed in an impossible dilemma by the consequences of a crime of which she was the victim. And what of Charisios, who has begun their marriage by becoming the father of a slave-prostitute's child, and whom she fully expects (821–3) to set up a separate establishment for the baby and its mother and divide his time between the two women, just as her father warned her he would? She describes him as 'unfortunate' (*atukhön*, 813; cf. 820 'I came to be his partner in life and in fortune') or, at worst, as having 'stumbled' (*eptaiken*, 821). Altogether she has displayed a quite extraordinary, even perverse degree of forbearance and self-effacement.[14] If her choice of words means anything, it means that in her eyes Charisios is in no way responsible for the birth of 'Habrotonon's baby' (an event which, on Aristotle's definition, must have occurred 'contrary to reasonable expectation' and/or be due to some 'external' cause), that Habrotonon was at least as much to be pitied as condemned, and that she herself is the guiltiest party of all. No wonder that Charisios, listening to all this, is affected to the core of his being!

Not that he comes anywhere near fully confronting his own guilt. On the contrary, he repeatedly describes himself as 'unfortunate' (*atukhôn*, 891; cf. 918) or as having 'stumbled' (*eptaikota*, 915) – the same terms that Pamphile had used – and twice he says that he and Pamphile have had 'similar' or 'the same' misfortunes (897, 915). By this he apparently means (cf. 896) that each of them has become the parent of a bastard child; he shows no awareness that this was a matter of far graver consequence for a woman – in physical pain, mental anguish and social stigma – than it could ever be for a man, nor that his 'misfortune', unlike Pamphile's, was caused by his own wilful, criminal act. He does not use the *adik-* root at all; he does use the *hamart-* root once (908), but only to say that he had formerly thought himself immune to *hamartēmata* (*anamartētos*), thus implying (but not actually stating!) that he now recognizes that he has 'erred'. Habrotonon got it right, four hundred lines earlier; and she it is who will presently tell Charisios that it doesn't matter any more, anyway – at least on the unquestioned assumption that marriage is a complete atonement for rape.

The Next Twenty-three Centuries

Menander, as we have seen, was only moderately successful at the Athenian festivals[1] during his lifetime. After his premature death, however, he quickly attained iconic status. The erection of a statue of him in the theatre area – the first time a *comic* poet had been so honoured – may have had a political motivation (see Ch. 1, p. 3), but the tendency to 'canonize' Menander was not reversed under the democratic regime of 287–61. Indeed it may well have been in this period that a series of mural paintings of scenes from Menander's plays (including *Epitrepontes*) was commissioned, which has been plausibly postulated as the source of many later artistic images, including murals from Pompeii and mosaics from Mytilene and elsewhere (see Nervegna 2013: 122–69).

At some point in the first half of the third century, the one-off performances of 'old' plays which had been a feature of the Athenian festival programmes since 386 (for tragedy; rather later for comedy) were replaced by regular competitions parallel to those in which new plays were performed, and we possess a fragmentary inscription from 255/4 recording such a contest (*Supplementum Epigraphicum Graecum* 26.208). 'Old' plays may have been defined simply as those composed by dead poets, since one of the entries for this contest was a play by Philemon, who (though twenty years senior to Menander) had died only in 263/2. Both his *Ptōchē (The Beggar Woman)* and Menander's *Phasma (The Apparition)* were defeated on this occasion by the *Misanthrōpoi (The Misanthropes)*[2] of Diphilus, later regarded as the third of the canonical triad of New Comic poets (corresponding to Aristophanes, Cratinus and Eupolis in Old Comedy). With the proliferation of dramatic festivals elsewhere in the much-expanded Greek world, many of which had contests for the performance of 'old' plays, from 200 BC (if not earlier) until AD 200 (if not later) there was probably never a year that did not see at least one, or more usually more than one, production of a Menandrian play somewhere in the *oikoumenē* (see Nervegna 2013: 11–110); and during the whole of that time, and beyond, comic dramatists composing new plays normally composed them to a Menandrian pattern (Nervegna 2013: 116–19).[3] Even in AD 362, when the emperor Julian, seeking to re-establish Graeco-Roman paganism as the religion of the empire, forbade Christians to teach classical literature, and the rhetorician (and future bishop) Apollinari(u)s of Laodicea set out to create off his own bat a new corpus of poetry in the classical genres fit for Christian students to read, the comedies he wrote were 'fashioned after the plays of Menander' (Sozomenus, *Ecclesiastical History* 5.18.2).

So had been many comedies written in Latin, ever since the third century BC. Early Roman comedy, represented for us by the works of Plautus, though based on Greek New Comedy, was a rumbustious genre, often more concerned to keep its public amused than to maintain fictive verisimilitude, and while the chorus is mostly either non-existent or inactive, this is more than made up for by the singing of individual characters, which can make a play of Plautus into something very like a musical. Even so, at least three of Plautus' twenty-one known plays are adaptations of Menander.[4] His successor Terence (active 166–59 BC) kept much more closely to the form and spirit of his Greek models, and found Menander extremely congenial; four of his six plays are based on Menandrian originals, and in contrast with Plautus' practice he retained the original titles[5] and even once (*Eunuchus* 19–20) makes a prologue-speaker say 'we are going to perform the *Eunuchus* of Menander'.

To judge by the number of surviving papyri, Menander was more read than any other poet except Homer, Hesiod and Euripides.[6] And *Epitrepontes* appears to have been one of his most popular plays. It has more papyri identified than any other play of Menander except *Misoumenos*.[7] And features of it are referred to casually in other texts, as if familiarity with *Epitrepontes* were something that could be counted on among educated Greeks (and educated Romans too). Cassius Dio

(60.29.3; third century AD) tells the following anecdote about Polybius, a powerful freedman at the court of the emperor Claudius:

> When an actor in the theatre delivered that much-quoted line 'A slave who prospers is an intolerable fellow' (Menander fr. 441) and the whole audience looked at Polybius . . . he shouted out that the same poet had also written 'Even those who were once goatherds have become kings'[8] (*Epitr.* 333, slightly misquoted); but Claudius did him no harm.

And as late as the sixth century AD the rhetorician Choricius of Gaza (32.2.73) can write:

> Or among the characters created by Menander, does Moschion predispose us to rape unmarried girls, *Chairestratos to fall in love with a harp-girl*, Knemon to be cantankerous, or Smikrines – the one who is afraid that something in his house may have been carried away by the smoke – to be money-grubbers?

There might, of course, have been another play of Menander in which another young man named Chairestratos falls in love with another harp-girl, but it is not very likely: Menander mentions harp-girls (*psaltriai*) only once (that we know of) outside *Epitrepontes*, and then merely as one item in a long list of luxuries; and his only other known character named Chairestratos, in *Aspis*, is an old man, though his ethical values are as sound as those of his counterpart in *Epitrepontes*. If the reference is indeed to *Epitrepontes*, it is striking that the Chairestratos-Habrotonon subplot, which is not at all prominent during most of *Epitrepontes*, is expected to be as well known as the character of Knemon in *Dyskolos*, or of one of Menander's numerous rapists named Moschion.[9]

There was never a fixed canon of select plays by Menander, as there was for Aeschylus, Sophocles, Euripides and Aristophanes,[10] and paradoxically this may have militated against the survival of his works: for any given intensity of interest in an author, the more different works of his were being read and copied, the fewer the copies that were being made of any particular work. Other factors also told against the survival of Menander. He had never been considered difficult enough to require a detailed exegetical commentary (N. G. Wilson 1983: 20; Blume 2010: 16), and none of our many papyri has more than the occasional annotation. His Greek was not quite what was regarded as the purest Attic (Blanchard 1997; Tribulato 2014). As Sebastiana Nervegna (2013: 259–60) has stressed, his plays did not serve well to introduce the young to the glories of ancient Greek history or myth. Too often, on the other hand, they did serve to introduce them to some of the seamier aspects of ancient Greek life (Easterling 1995). And since at least the first century, there had been another 'Menander' in the schools: a collection of worthy maxims, each occupying one iambic line, some actually by Menander (often with modifications to make them fitter for general use), some by other dramatists and even prose authors, a considerable number manifestly created by schoolmasters.[11] This collection existed in many different versions and eventually in several languages, and this, not the comic dramas, was what 'Menander' meant to the Byzantine schoolboy and his teacher alike.

The plays themselves apparently ceased to be copied. We have no manuscript of any Menandrian play later than the early seventh century AD, and in several cases old copies were erased and the parchment recycled for a different text (usually a theological one, and not always in Greek).[12] All that remained of the real Menander were several hundred quotations made by various ancient authors, ranging from a single word to about twenty lines; in addition the West, though not Byzantium, had the adaptations of Menander made by Roman dramatists, especially Terence. The Renaissance united these two streams of knowledge; but direct modern acquaintance with Menandrian play-scripts only began in 1844, and remained very limited for another sixty-three years. Both in 1844 and in 1907, *Epitrepontes* was in the forefront.

In 1844, the German biblical scholar, Constantin von Tischendorf (1815–74), came to St Catherine's monastery on Mount Sinai – where fifteen years later he was to discover the famous Codex Sinaiticus of the Greek Bible – and found there, among other things, what we now know to be a leaf from a copy of *Epitrepontes* (and another leaf from a different play). But they were glued into the cover of another book, and he could only read one side of each leaf. So he did, and took a transcript away with him. And nothing happened; the transcript remained unpublished. As a friend of his, the Dutch scholar C. G. Cobet, wrote after his death (Cobet 1876: 293):

> 'Tischendorf, who was entirely absorbed in seeking out and investigating manuscripts of the Holy Scriptures, made no systematic search for classical material of this kind, and discussed it only incidentally.'

In fact he had been intending to publish his new classical discoveries eventually, but he died before he could bring this project to fruition.

Several years after Tischendorf's visit, Porfiry Uspensky (1804–85), then the head of the Russian Church Mission in Jerusalem, rediscovered these leaves at the monastery and was able to separate them from the book cover, eventually taking this and many other manuscripts back to St Petersburg. And again nothing happened; the leaves remained in Uspensky's private collection until he sold it to the Imperial Library in 1883.

Meanwhile, however, something else had happened. In 1876, a year or two after Tischendorf's death, Cobet published in the journal *Mnemosyne* (of which he was senior editor) the nine-page article from which the extract quoted above was taken, with the title (in Latin) 'Unpublished Fragments of Menander'. Cobet printed Tischendorf's 1844 fragments, and showed that they came from two plays of Menander, one of which he thought (wrongly) that he could identify (it is now known to be *Phasma*). He also wrote some valuable notes on the other fragment, but made no suggestion as to what play it might have come from. Tischendorf's transcript of it contained nineteen lines; subsequent examination has added small fragments of three more.[13]

It was not until 1891 that the Sinai fragments were published in full, in a study by Viktor Jernstedt entitled, in honour of Uspensky, *The Porphyrian Fragments of Attic Comedy*. Now about twice as much text was available, but it still could not be established which play it was from, and the new publication made little impact, in part perhaps because it was written in Russian rather than in, say, German or Latin.[14]

Just about this time there began a veritable explosion in the rediscovery of ancient manuscripts preserved in the dry soil of Egypt, including in the first few years several odes by the highly reputed, but hitherto all but completely lost, lyric poet Bacchylides, almost the whole text of Aristotle's (or one of his students') account of the Athenian constitution and its history, and many other exciting finds. These included, from 1898 onwards, portions of some plays of Menander, but none was very extensive (the longest was about 87 lines), and there was nothing to throw substantial light on the St Petersburg fragments.[15]

The great breakthrough for Menander, and for *Epitrepontes*, came in 1907 with the publication by Gustave Lefebvre of a manuscript found at Aphroditopolis (Gebelein in Upper Egypt), now in the Museum of Egyptian Antiquities in Cairo, which turned out to contain parts of six plays, five of them by Menander. After thirteen centuries in the shadows, Menander had returned to the light in the form of real scripts that could be studied and maybe, with a bit of restoration, even performed on stage. And the best preserved of these was *Epitrepontes*.

The manuscript, which had been written in the fifth century AD, proved to have had a chequered history. Some hundred years after it had been written, its then owner, a man named Flavius Dioscorus, had taken its leaves apart and used them as covers for his business documents. When those that could be found were put together again, they turned out to contain parts of six ancient comedies.[16] One of these was the *Demes* of the Old Comic dramatist Eupolis; this text must have been quite a rarity at the time when it was copied, for it is at least a century later than any other papyrus of an Old Comedy that is not one of the eleven select plays of Aristophanes. The other five were all by Menander. Four were soon identified as *Hērōs (The Hero), Epitrepontes, Perikeiromene* and *Samia*; the fifth has never been identified at all and is still known only as 'the unidentified play' (*Fabula Incerta*).[17]

The identification of *Epitrepontes* was easy: the manuscript contained a number of passages which were quoted by various later ancient authors as coming from *Epitrepontes*. What was more, the very first preserved scene was that of the arbitration, to which the play owed its name. It was now possible to read what looked like almost the whole of Act II and most of Act III; Acts IV and V were scrappier, but by great good fortune the codex preserves the three scenes in which Pamphile, Charisios and Smikrines successively learn the truth about the baby.

Before long it was perceived that one of the two leaves in St Petersburg also belonged to the same play. The name Charisios (168) was a link,[18] and the situation fitted (a father-in-law complaining about the squandering of his daughter's dowry, exactly as Charisios' father-in-law does later in the play). The fragment included a break between two acts, and as the ends of Acts II, III and IV were already identifiable, this had to be the end of Act I. The lines on these two pages are still the only parts of Act I that exist in a continuously readable form.

Epitrepontes, though far from complete, was now much the best preserved play of Menander, and it duly became, in 1925, the first to receive a separate scholarly edition with commentary, the editor being the greatest Greek literary scholar of his time, Ulrich von Wilamowitz-Moellendorff. At that time only one further papyrus was known in addition to the Sinai fragments and the Cairo codex, and it was not until 1983 (with *Oxyrhynchus Papyri* 3532–3) that new portions of the play's text began to come to light; since then, as we have seen, there have been significant accretions in all five Acts, though we still do not know, for example, who the god was that spoke the prologue (indeed we have no direct evidence that there actually was such a prologue), or how soon the audience was made aware of Chairestratos' feelings for Habrotonon, or whether Habrotonon gained the freedom she had so dearly longed for.

Gilbert Murray (1866–1957), perhaps the greatest interpreter (in several media) of ancient Greek drama to the English-speaking public, brought out in 1945 a translation of *Epitrepontes*, which was later twice broadcast by the BBC. He had no more papyrus evidence to work with than Wilamowitz had had, and much of his script was inevitably restoration, some of it the product of what can at best be termed wishful thinking (for example, Habrotonon is discovered to be Pamphile's long-lost sister and so can be married to Chairestratos).[19] Nevertheless this, together with Murray's earlier (1942) translation of *Perikeiromene,* was a bold and worthwhile attempt to draw Menander to the attention of a wider public.

The first modern production of (part of) a play of Menander took place, fittingly, at Athens on 16 April 1908, when the arbitration scene was performed (in a modern Greek translation) at the Parnassos Philological Society (Kiritsi 2019). There have been relatively few performances since. The Oxford *Archive of Performances of Greek and Roman Drama*[20] records just 21 separate productions; by comparison, the least popular play of Aristophanes in modern times, *Wealth,* registers 50 productions since 1907, the almost equally little-known *Peace* 100, and *Lysistrata* no fewer than 350. Menander does not sell easily in the modern theatre; he rarely goes out of his way to earn a laugh as Aristophanes constantly does, his treatment of rape is generally and rightly felt to be abhorrent,[21] and in *Epitrepontes* itself nothing is seen until Act IV of the two characters whose fate is central to the play, their reunion then occurs offstage, and they never exchange a word.[22]

By far the most successful modern production of *Epitrepontes* was that created by the Greek translator Tassos Roussos and director Spyros Evangelatos in 1980 (Figure 3; see Kiritsi 2014), which was presented first at Epidaurus and then at many other venues in Greece and also in Italy, the United States, Australia and Germany. The plot ran on continuously, but each of the five acts was set in a different historical and theatrical era, with costumes and acting styles to match – Hellenistic Greece, Renaissance Italy (the Commedia dell'Arte), seventeenth-century France (Molière), Victorian England (Oscar Wilde and his contemporaries), and mid-twentieth-century Greece (cinematic melodramas) – the latter four all being genres that are either ultimately descended from, or in important respects parallel to, Greek New Comedy. A certain dose of relatively broad comedy was added, particularly in the Onesimos-Karion scene in Act I (where even less of Menander's text was known in 1980 than now) and also, more surprisingly, in Act IV where Charisios, making his first appearance,[23] comes on stage drunk. Before that first appearance Charisios had been, if anything, an even bigger offstage presence than he was in Menander's original. Few concessions were made to the mores of modern society. A touch or two of presentation and language is used to suggest that Pamphile is in love with Charisios as well as he with her, and this may have made it more plausible that she could ignore in her joy the crime he had committed against her at a time when neither knew who the other was. Onesimos, especially in Act IV, is more servant than slave, and can be outspokenly critical of his master to his face.[24] But fundamentally the Roussos-Evangelatos play is Menander's play (or rather Menander's play so far as it was known or reconstructible in 1980) and it testifies that Menander's drama can after all be made appealing to a late twentieth-century public. And by its structure, it helps to remind us of the unique role that Greek New Comedy, and Menander as its leading exponent, played in the history of European drama: 'the fundamental plot elements of Menander's comedy recur throughout the history of Western drama' (Witzke 2019), from the days of Plautus and Terence to the cinematic 'romcoms', and TV 'soaps' and 'sitcoms', of our own time.

Figure 3 A scene from Act III of *Epitrepontes* in the 1980 production by Tassos Roussos and Spyros Evangelatos.

And of Menander's plays, *Epitrepontes* is perhaps the finest that we know; if it was written late in his career, as now seems likely (see Ch. 1, p. 5) one can well understand why Plutarch felt that at the time of his premature death his abilities were still improving, and grieve for the dramas that fate did not permit him to compose.

Appendix: Texts, Translations and Commentaries

Texts

Owing to the continuing identification of new papyrus fragments, even the most recent edition of *Epitrepontes* (Blanchard 2013; with introduction, French translation, and annotation on the modest scale of the Budé series) is not fully up to date. The editions of Furley 2009a (aimed more at the specialist) and Ireland 2010a (aimed more at the student) lack only the additional fragments of the Michigan papyrus published by Römer since 2012 (and Furley 2021) has fully updated the relevant portions of his edition); both include translations and valuable commentaries, and their introductions complement each other. The handiest 'complete' edition of Menander remains the Oxford Classical Text of Sandbach 1972/1990, but this is now badly out of date and a replacement is sorely needed.

Translations

For the serious student, the most useful English translation of *Epitrepontes* is that of Ireland 2010a; Furley 2009a is of equal quality but is limited to passages well enough preserved to be continuously translatable, whereas Ireland aims to offer a rendering of every complete word that survives or that can be restored with reasonable confidence. Arnott 1979–2000: i 379–526 is an excellent verse translation, but has now become very incomplete. The best single-volume Menander translation (of all the plays of which a significant quantity of continuous text is preserved, plus some of the longer ancient quotations and a few papyrus fragments whose attribution to Menander is uncertain) is Balme and Brown 2001; they offer supplements (printed in italics) to bridge some of the gaps in the text, but these should not be regarded as anything but illustrative possibilities.

Commentaries

The most exhaustive commentary on *Epitrepontes* is that of Martina 2000 (in Italian); supplementary studies are presented in Martina 2016: i 74–181, 324–32. Best in English is the combination of Furley 2009a (+ Furley 2021) and Ireland 2010a; there is also still much of value in Gomme & Sandbach 1973: 289–384.

Glossary

agōn modern term for a set-piece debate between two characters, such as is found in a majority of Aristophanes' surviving plays and, in a somewhat different form, is also frequent in Euripides. The arbitration scene in *Epitrepontes* has many of the characteristics of an *agon*, and obeys the rule that the first contender to speak will be the loser.

archōn the principal magistrate of the Athenian state, who among his other duties presided over the City Dionysia, and who gave his name to his year of office (thus Menander was born *epi archontos Sōsigenous* 'in the archonship of Sosigenes' (342/1 BC)).

codex a manuscript consisting, like a modern book, of leaves stacked one above another and sewn together along one side. The codex (typically of parchment) gradually replaced the (sc)roll (typically of papyrus) between the first and fourth centuries.

deme (*dēmos*) one of about 140 districts into which Athens' home territory was divided. Every male citizen, upon coming of age, was registered as a member of the deme to which his father had belonged (even if the family had long ceased to live there), and his deme affiliation was part of his full official name; thus Menander was officially known as *Menandros Diopeithous Kēphisieus* 'Menander son of Diopeithes of Cephisia'.

Dionysia (also called Great or City Dionysia) the most important Athenian festival of Dionysus, held in the month of Elaphebolion (March/April) and including competitions in comedy and tragedy.

dowry (*proix*) sum of money transferred, together with a bride, by her father or guardian to her husband; repayable if the marriage was terminated otherwise than by death.

eisodos one of two passages leading into the *orchestra* at its right and left, used for the entrance and exit of the chorus and of characters coming from or going to places other than those represented by (parts of) the *skene*.

ekkyklēma a device by means of which an indoor scene could be presented to the audience (available to Menander but not used in *Epitrepontes*).

ephebe (*ephēbos*) a male citizen aged eighteen to twenty undergoing a civic and military apprenticeship in semi-segregated conditions.

epiklēros the daughter of a man who has died leaving no son. She was required to marry the nearest relative who put in a claim, and the whole of her father's estate was put in her husband's hands until a son of the marriage came of age.

Hellenistic the Hellenistic period of Greek history (so called because during it many non-Greek peoples were 'hellenized' by acquiring the Greek language and many aspects of Greek culture) is usually taken to extend from the death of Alexander the Great (323 BC) to the absorption of the last major Hellenistic kingdom (Egypt) into the Roman empire (30 BC).

hetaira the generic term for a female sex-worker; sometimes used to refer more specifically to those who were free (in contrast to *pornē* which typically denoted a slave prostitute).

hybris behaviour manifesting a contemptuous disregard for the rights or dignity of another; at Athens a crime with no fixed penalty, the jury being required to choose between prosecution and defence proposals.

Hypothesis an annotation prefixed to a text, giving factual (or purportedly factual) information about the text. In the case of dramatic texts this most often includes a synopsis of the plot and/or particulars of the first production (date, result of competition, etc.).

iambic poetry a genre which flourished especially in the seventh and sixth centuries BC. The poet often spoke directly in the first person, and engaged in invective against those whom he presented as enemies.

kyrios the person who had legal responsibility for the maintenance and protection of a woman or minor, and who acted on her/his behalf in matters (such as legal proceedings) in which women and minors could not act themselves. The *kyrios* of an unmarried girl was normally her father; of a wife, her husband; of a widowed mother, one or more of her sons.

Lenaea an Athenian festival of Dionysus, held in the month of Gamelion (January/February) and including competitions in comedy and tragedy.

metoikos (often anglicized as 'metic') a free non-citizen permanently resident in Attica (the territory constituting the *polis* of Athens).

nothos a bastard. The child of an Athenian citizen father was a *nothos* (feminine *nothē*) unless his/her mother was (1) of citizen status and (2) lawfully married to the father by the time of, or at least very soon after, the child's birth, so that the baby could be presented to his/her father's phratry (q.v.) as legitimate.

oikoumenē literally 'the inhabited (world)'; in practice, the Greek-speaking (later, Greek- or Latin-speaking) world.

orchēstra level space between the elevated stage and the audience seating, traditionally occupied by the chorus of a play (or, at other times, by choruses taking part in non-dramatic competitions).

palimpsest a manuscript whose original text has been erased and another text written over it.

pallakē a woman cohabiting with a free man in a relationship which is not a marriage (normally because the woman is not of citizen status) but has no fixed expiry date (unlike the fixed-term fidelity contracts sometimes made by *hetairai*), though it can be terminated by either party without formality and without notice.

papyrus term applied to any surviving manuscript, or fragment of one, written in antiquity (before about A D 700) on papyrus, parchment or similar material. Most papyri have been preserved in the dry soil of Egypt.

parodos (1) the first utterance, or sequence of utterances, of a dramatic chorus at its entrance; represented in the scripts of New Comedy, like other choral performances, merely by the note *khorou*. (2) in later usage, = *eisodos*.

phallus a large artificial penis. Outsize phalli were carried in religious processions, especially at festivals of Dionysus, and smaller ones (still more than life-size) were worn as part of the regular costume of male characters in Old and some Middle Comedy.

phratry a group of families which assembled annually at the festival of the Apaturia, when children born to members during the preceding year were presented to the phratry; proof of such presentation was regarded as valuable evidence of citizen status.

polis a city-state; an autonomous political entity with a territory centred on a (usually fortified) town.

pornē a prostitute. The term typically denotes a slave owned by a *pornoboskos* (see next entry), but can be applied disparagingly to any sex-worker.

pornoboskos a man or woman who owned slave sex-workers and hired them to clients.

protagonist (*prōtagōnistēs*) the principal actor in a play.

skēnē the back-stage building, in New Comedy usually representing two private houses (in *Epitrepontes* those of Charisios and Chairestratos).

talent (*talanton*) as a sum of money, one talent equalled 6,000 drachmae.

Notes

Chapter 1

1 Now an upmarket suburb of Athens, about 12 km north-east of the city centre. Its municipal flag features a wreathed head purporting to be that of 'Menander the Cephisian'; unfortunately it credits him with a thick if well-trimmed beard, whereas his numerous ancient images (Nervegna 2013: 14–16, 122–30) always show him clean-shaven. We do not know whether Menander ever actually lived at Cephisia: deme membership depended not on one's own place of residence, but on that of one's male-line ancestor in 508/7 BC.

2 Dates given in this form (000/0 or 000/00) denote Athenian calendar years; these began and ended in the summer, usually in what would now be July.

3 According to a tradition which may go back to his near-contemporary Callimachus (fr. 396 Pfeiffer), he was drowned while swimming off the Peiraeus.

4 His insurrection, we are told, disrupted the City Dionysia and prevented the performance of Menander's play *Imbrioi* (*The Men from Imbros*) (*Oxyrhynchus Papyrus* 1255).

5 On the history and politics of Athens in the early Hellenistic period, see Habicht 1997: 36–123, Bayliss 2011.

6 Two new tribes, named after the 'saviour gods' Antigonus and Demetrius, were added at that time to the ten tribes created by Cleisthenes two centuries before; they were abolished in 200 when Athens declared war on Demetrius' descendant Philip V. By then a further tribe had been created in honour of Ptolemy III of Egypt (224), and the same tribute was paid in 200 to Attalus of Pergamum and in AD 126 to the emperor Hadrian.

7 Demetrius of Phalerum is reported to have said that far from abolishing democracy, he had put it back on its feet (Strabo 9.1.20).

8 Potter 1987: 491–5 argues that this Telesphorus was actually a cousin of Demetrius of Phalerum; but Telesphorus is not found as an Athenian name before the second century AD. To be sure, this man can hardly be the general who rebelled against Antigonus in 312 (Diodorus Siculus 19.74–5,

87), but he could perfectly well be an undistinguished (and otherwise unrecorded) member of the Antigonid family who had come to Athens in his cousin's entourage and who admired Menander as a dramatist. In any case, as things turned out, Menander's seemingly perilous position proved secure: of those associates of Demetrius of Phalerum who stayed in Athens after his fall and stood trial, not one was convicted (Philochorus *FGrH* 328 F 66).

9   In the end he will discover that he is the father of the very man whose pleas to the assembly he had disparaged. It is striking that his sentiments now appear to be echoed almost precisely by a sympathetic character, Pamphile, in *Epitr.* 810–13 (see Furley 2021) which was most probably produced in the 290s (see p. 5) – though Pamphile is not thinking about politics (with which, as a woman, she has no concern) but merely trying to dissuade her father from believing all the tales circulating about Charisios' allegedly scandalous behaviour.

10 Iversen 2011, however, argues on the basis of an epigram by the Roman poet Martial (14.187) that Menander's first play was actually *Thais* and that *Orge* was the play with which he scored his first Dionysia victory in 315.

11 This does not necessarily mean that no one before him had produced a play when under twenty: the ephebic system in its fully developed form had been created quite recently, by a law of 334 (Sommerstein 1996: 53–9).

12 Menander was by no means the first comic dramatist to compose many more plays than he could have produced in the Theatre of Dionysus. Among Middle Comic dramatists, the output of Alexis is reported as 245.

13 The *Monosticha* have been edited by Jaekel 1964 and Pernigotti 2008. The only modern English translation is that of Edmonds 1961: 900–89 (where many lines firmly established in the textual tradition have been arbitrarily relegated to footnotes).

14 Perhaps even more. The Loeb Classical Library edition of Aeschylus (Sommerstein 2008) contains, in its three volumes, 1,528 pages, including those designated by Roman numerals; that of Menander (Arnott 1979–2000) contains 1,740; and since these editions were published there has been much more new Menandrian than Aeschylean material.

Chapter 2

1 The classic study of New Comedy (and its Roman offshoot) is Hunter 1985; more recent overviews are Ireland 2010b and Scafuro 2014a (which should be read together with Scafuro 2014b). On production and performance aspects of Menandrian drama, the most comprehensive treatment is the combination of Green 2010 and Csapo 2010, though both authors cover the whole history of Greek comedy and Green needs to be updated in regard to the theatrical environment (Papastamati-von Moock 2014); on masks and costumes see also the detailed analysis by Webster et al. 1995. On Menander specifically, a new or updated book-length general introduction in English is badly needed, such is the quantity of new papyri that have appeared since the time of Webster 1974, Goldberg 1980, or even Zagagi 1994.

2 Presumably in speaking of 'probable' events Aristotle is not thinking of the situations which, as it were, generate the plot, and which often, both in comedy and in tragedy, involve highly implausible coincidences (such as that Charisios should unknowingly marry the very woman whom he had raped four months earlier), but the decisions and actions of the characters in response to these situations ('what . . . will inevitably or probably be said or done') and their consequences.

3 i.e. Archilochus, Hipponax and others in their tradition; the iambic genre, like Old Comedy, was notorious for the prominence of invective against individuals. Earlier (in chapter 5) Aristotle had credited Crates (active *c.* 450–430) with being the first Athenian comic dramatist who 'abandoned the iambic style and created plots of a universal nature': and indeed the surviving fragments of Crates, which amount to 60–70 lines in all, contain not one reference to any contemporary individual.

4 His surviving fragments, some 183 lines in all (see now Apostolakis 2019), contain no fewer than forty-eight such references.

5 Thus ancient commentators quoting comic parallels for the language or content of a passage of Aristophanes cite Old Comedy almost exclusively; Athenaeus (second/third century AD), compiling what may be called an encyclopaedic dictionary of banqueting, quotes Middle Comedy more often than Old and New taken together (and supplies three-quarters of all surviving Middle Comedy quotations); and the fifth-century anthologist

John of Stobi (Stobaeus) quotes New Comedy (for which he is the
largest single source) more often than Old and Middle taken together.

6 Another common theme seems to have been the reunion of long-
separated siblings; this provided the main plot-line in the Greek plays that
lie behind Plautus' *Captivi (The Captives)* and *Menaechmi (The Two
Menaechmuses)*, and an important secondary theme in *Perikeiromene*
(where a wry twist is given to it as Moschion discovers to his chagrin that
the girl with whom he is in love is his long-lost twin sister!) Comedy was
also still occasionally used as a vehicle for political polemic: Philippides
(frr. 25, 26) launched one or more attacks on Stratocles, the chief Athenian
supporter of Demetrius Poliorcetes, and Archedicus (fr. 4) upon the
democratic champion Demochares.

7 This paragraph, and the next five, are adapted from Sommerstein 2013:
6–10.

8 A *hetaira* ('female companion') is any woman who makes herself (or, if a
slave, is made by her owner) sexually available for reward. At one extreme
of the spectrum is the slave who is made to work in a brothel or (like
Habrotonon in *Epitrepontes*) is hired out for the pleasure of partygoers
(and who may be disparagingly termed a *pornē*, 'whore'); at the other
is the woman whose attractions and accomplishments enable her to make
her own terms for becoming the permanent or semi-permanent, and
faithful, partner of a well-to-do man (though she too can be called a *pornē*
by her or her partner's enemies: cf. [Demosthenes] 59.114). See Brown
1993; Davidson 1997; Faraone & McClure 2006; E. E. Cohen 2015;
Glazebrook 2015.

9 Possibly they retired to an inconspicuous position at the edge of the
orchestra; there is some reason to believe that choruses sometimes did this
even in Aristophanes' time (see Sommerstein 1990: 202 on Aristophanes,
Lysistrata 907).

10 The piper who accompanied the choral interludes may also have played
during, and given a stricter rhythm to, at least some of the passages
written in eight-foot metres (iambic or trochaic tetrameters); in
Epitrepontes, however, no such passages survive, and there may well never
have been any.

11 In *Epitrepontes* this probably happened before and after the 'delayed
prologue', spoken by a divine being, which most scholars believe formed
the middle portion of Act I; it also occurs at 877/8 (exeunt Pamphile and

Habrotonon; enter Onesimos) and at 1060/1 (exit Charisios; enter Smikrines and Sophrone).

12 Whereas in Aristophanes there are several scenes involving four speaking characters (see MacDowell 1994).

13 In many plays, including *Epitrepontes*, this would involve the splitting of one or more parts between different actors; we know that dramatists and audiences found this acceptable, since Sophocles had done it in his last tragedy, *Oedipus at Colonus* (written 406, produced posthumously 401), some sixty years before Menander was born. Furley 2009a:16–17 offers a casting of *Epitrepontes* that minimizes part-splitting: only two roles are divided between actors, and neither is taken by different actors in consecutive Acts. This casting rests, however, on the dubious assumption (see Ch. 4, pp. 39–43) that Charisios does not appear in Act V. It is certainly plausible enough that the two biggest parts, those of Smikrines and Onesimos, were each played by the same actor throughout, the protagonist probably taking that of Smikrines who appears in the two most memorable scenes (the arbitration in Act II, and the confrontation with Pamphile in Act IV); on the other hand the most sympathetic characters are Syriskos and Pamphile, each of whom has one very long and moving speech, and an actor who took these parts could take at least two others as well and thereby demonstrate great versatility.

14 The third door, in the centre, could also represent the entrance to another kind of interior space (e.g. a cave-shrine in *Dyskolos*, a temple in *Leukadia* [*The Woman from Leucas*]).

15 There are virtually no citizen males of intermediate age in New Comedy, just as there are virtually no children who have passed babyhood but not reached adolescence.

16 Cited by Turner 1979: 108.

17 In Aristophanes' *Knights* (319–21), for example, a character complains about the bad leather prepared by the 'tanner' Paphlagon (a caricature of the politician Cleon): 'before I got to Pergase', he says, 'I was swimming in my shoes'. Pergase was about 13 km from Athens, and it was not necessarily the speaker's final destination.

18 Daos and Syriskos appear only in Acts II and III, and in these acts Smikrines does not arrive from, or depart to, his home. In Act II he enters from Charisios' house (where he had gone to see how things were with his daughter, 161–3) and leaves at about 370 for the city (cf. 577–8); he returns

thence half-way through Act III, at the end of which he goes back into Charisios' house intending to take his daughter away.

19 Our ancient sources give varying and inconsistent descriptions of alleged conventions relating the two *eisodoi* to three basic offstage directions – the city (or Agora), the port (not relevant in *Epitrepontes*) and the countryside; in fact no fixed convention can account for the ways in which offstage directions are actually deployed in the plays. Some of the sources speak of rotating devices of triangular cross-section, called *periaktoi*, close to each of the *eisodoi*, which could indicate the *eisodos*'s current function (their three faces perhaps displaying respectively an urban scene, a rural scene, and a ship at sea); this is plausible enough, but we cannot tell when the device was introduced.

20 Thus in Aeschylus' lost *Myrmidons*, at the start of which Achilles sat veiled and silent for a long time before eventually speaking in reply to his old tutor Phoenix (Aeschylus fr. 132b.6–9), the chorus at the very outset made it clear that he was sitting inside his hut (Aeschylus fr. 131.3–4).

21 The only clear case in a surviving text is *Dyskolos* 690–758 (Knemon in bed following a serious accident).

22 On monologues in Menander see Blundell 1980, Scafuro 2014b: 229–31.

23 The slave on the left-hand side of the Mytilene mosaic (Figure 2) appears to be wearing trousers (a decidedly 'barbarian' garment), as does the (African) cook in the companion mosaic illustrating *Samia*.

Chapter 3

1 In this it is almost unique. Until about AD 300 Eupolis (a contemporary of Aristophanes) and Cratinus (who was a generation older, but competed with Aristophanes and Eupolis in his last years) were quite widely read, but after that date we possess hardly any papyrus fragments of any Old Comedies except the eleven plays of Aristophanes that survived into, and through, the Middle Ages.

2 The exact number depends on whether *Berlin Papyrus* 21142 is regarded as a fragment of *Epitrepontes*, to which it has sometimes been assigned on account of the presence in it of the name Charisios, which is not known to have occurred in any other comedy. The editors of *Poetae Comici Graeci* cautiously treated the fragment as anonymous (*comica adespota* 1121).

3 One of these (F 7 = lines 793–6) is now paralleled by three papyri, but its full text could not be securely restored even from the three taken together.

4 The plays by Plautus based on Menandrian originals are *Bacchides* (parts of which can be directly compared with a papyrus fragment of its source *Dis Exapaton [The Double Deception]*), *Cistellaria* (based on *Synaristosai*) and *Stichus*; those by Terence (who kept the original titles) are *Adelphoe [The Brothers]*, *Andria [The Woman from Andros]*, *Eunuchus [The Eunuch]*, and *Heauton Timōrumenos [The Man who Punished Himself]*.

Chapter 4

1 From a passage by the sophist Themistius (fourth century AD) in which the words 'there's nothing more pleasurable than knowing everything', quoted elsewhere in conjunction with a statement that the speaker shares Onesimos' inquisitiveness about matters that are not his business, are associated with 'the comic cook' and with the name Karion; and now also from some marginal speaker-indications in *Oxyrhynchus Papyrus* 4936 (column ii, lines 3 and 6).

2 Of the first 365 lines preserved in the Cairo codex (218–582) no fewer than 352 are spoken by these four slaves. On Menander's presentation of slaves and slavery, see Proffitt 2011; Konstan 2013; Cox 2013; Marshall 2013; Vester 2013; Bathrellou 2014a.

3 *Trophimos* ('the one being reared') was originally the term used by slaves to refer to the *son* of their master. When the master died, his son would become 'the master' (*despotes*), but often, particularly if he was still a young man, the slaves would continue to call him *trophimos*. Hence the use of this term here hints at the possible appearance of a sixth character, Charisios' father, who in fact will never be mentioned (so far as we know) and whom, if we think about him at all later in the play, we will presume to be dead.

4 Babies who are born shortly before, or (as quite often happens) actually during, the action of a New Comedy to mothers who are, or are later discovered to be, of citizen status, are invariably first-borns and invariably male.

5 The surviving text does not make Sophrone's status clear. It has usually been assumed (as by Arnott 1979: 385 and Ireland) that she is a slave of

Smikrines, who certainly speaks to her in 1062–75 as though he had an
unlimited right to inflict on her any ill-treatment up to and including
death; but this would make it difficult for her to be involved in the
exposure of Pamphile's baby. Slaves who served as nurses were often set
free in their old age (e.g. *Samia* 236–8, [Demosthenes] 47.55), and
Sophrone may therefore be a freedwoman living on her own and making
regular and welcome visits to her old nursling Pamphile; it is not
surprising that a man of Smikrines' temperament should treat her as
though she were still his slave.

6   He could have done this simply by ordering her to leave his house
    – though he would then have been legally obliged to return her dowry; see
    MacDowell 1978: 88.

7   In *Oxyrhynchus Papyrus* 4936 he is first named as a speaker at column ii
    line 8, but that is not necessarily the first time he spoke.

8   Both Habrotonon (437) and Smikrines (129–39) assume that Charisios is
    paying for the wine and the woman, even though he is not the host. Is this
    because he is the richer of the two or is he, as Smikrines alleges,
    squandering his wife's dowry money? A couple of factors favour the latter
    conclusion: (1) Smikrines' complaint that in spite of having received a
    four-talent dowry, Charisios has not 'regarded himself as his wife's servant'
    (134–5) may indicate that the dowry constitutes the bulk of his assets; (2)
    Chairestratos has at least one non-domestic slave (214–5) whereas
    Charisios has none that we know of. It does not follow that Charisios is
    what the average Athenian citizen would call a poor man; New Comedy
    regularly exaggerates the net worth of its citizen characters, as it
    exaggerates also the size of the dowries they give (Schaps 1979: 99).

9   Various guesses have been made as to his/her identity, but there is no
    evidence. Prologue-speaking deities in Menander are normally minor gods
    like Pan (*Dyskolos*) or personified abstractions like Tychē 'Chance' (*Aspis*)
    or Agnoia 'Ignorance, Misapprehension' (*Perikeiromene*). If one were to
    make a guess about a personification appropriate to *Epitrepontes*, one
    might think of Pistotēs, 'Faithfulness, Loyalty', which is conspicuously
    displayed by many of the characters and is largely responsible for the
    happy outcome (see Ch. 6); another possibility (Heap 2002/3: 98, Ireland
    2010a: 237) is Peithō, 'Persuasion' (cf. 555, 713, 1067, 1070), a goddess who
    smiles on Syriskos in the arbitration scene and on Habrotonon when she
    pretends to be the baby's mother, but emphatically not on Smikrines when

he tries to persuade his daughter to abandon her marriage. There is, however, some evidence that major deities like Aphrodite and Dionysus were sometimes brought on for this purpose (*comica adespota* 53, 1008), so one cannot completely rule out a figure like Artemis Tauropolos, on whose festival day, the Tauropolia, the baby was conceived. On divine prologues in Menander see Miles 2014; Ireland 2019a, b. On what is known or can be plausibly inferred about the Tauropolia, see Bathrellou 2012; she points out (pp. 170–8) that Habrotonon's description of Pamphile (480–90) in effect compares her to the leader of a maiden chorus dancing in honour of Artemis – a prestigious position but also, in myth and poetry (and later in the Greek novels), a sexually hazardous one. It is probably significant that two of the other three Menandrian rapes whose occasions we know also took place at festivals of Artemis.

10 The official ceremonies for this festival took place at Halai Araphenides on the east coast of Attica, but private celebrations need not have been confined to that locality.

11 Throughout New Comedy it is taken for granted that a child conceived, or even born, out of wedlock is made legitimate by the subsequent marriage of its parents, if they were both of citizen status and neither was married to a third person at any relevant time.

12 The prologue of *Aspis* occupies fifty-two lines, that of *Dyskolos* forty-nine; in *Perikeiromene* fifty-one lines of the prologue survive, with perhaps ten or fifteen having been lost at the beginning (cf. Gomme & Sandbach 1973: 467). The prologue of *Samia* was much longer (about ninety lines, of which fifty-seven survive in whole or in part; see Arnott 1999), but being delivered by a major human character it has not only an expository function but also that of laying bare the personality and character of the speaker, Moschion.

13 The conventional line-numbering for *Epitrepontes* was devised by A. W. Gomme in the 1950s; it is fairly satisfactory for the parts of the play included in the Cairo codex, but it probably underestimates the size of all the major gaps, especially the section between the end of the Tischendorf leaf (177) and the beginning of the Cairo codex (218); two papyri have already given us parts of forty-three lines from this section, and this certainly does not represent anything like the whole of it.

14 He himself is almost grotesquely stingy, reckoning (135–40) that twelve drachmas (the amount that Charisios is paying, per day, for the services of

Habrotonon) would be enough to feed a man for thirty-six days. Chairestratos' comment on this is 'Good calculation! Two obols [one-third of a drachma] a day – enough to keep a starving man supplied with barley gruel!'

15 It is a cliché of Middle and New Comedy (e.g. Menander frr. 296, 297, 802; Anaxandrides fr. 53.4–6; Plautus, *Asinaria* 87) that a wife who brings much more wealth into the marriage than her husband does can be expected to consider herself the head and master of the household; see Arnott 1996: 441–4. It is unusual, however, for the wife's father thus to assume, and proclaim, that subservience is his son-in-law's duty.

16 I suspect that he wanted some time alone to think about his feelings for Habrotonon, in particular perhaps how they might conflict with his friendship with Charisios. When he fears (131–3) that Smikrines may 'storm in [i.e. into Chairestratos' house] and wreck the loving', it will then be this love of his own that he has in mind.

17 So in the mid fourth century Phrastor of Aigilia dismissed his wife Phano, and refused to return her dowry, because he had come to believe that she was not of citizen status and therefore could not lawfully be married to a citizen. Stephanus, who claimed to be Phano's father, sued Phrastor for the dowry (more precisely, for an order to pay interest on it at the penal rate of 18 per cent), but Phrastor countered with a prosecution of Stephanus for giving Phano in marriage under the pretence that she was a citizen, and this forced Stephanus to come to terms, both lawsuits being withdrawn and Phrastor presumably retaining the dowry. See [Demosthenes] 59 (*Against Neaera*) 50–4.

18 Syriskos is what was called a *khōris oikōn*, a slave 'living independently': he has a home and family of his own, does what work he chooses, but is required to pay a fixed sum each month (called *apophora*, 380) to his master out of his earnings. Nothing shows for certain whether Daos is in this category; Syriskos may be his superior socially as well as morally.

19 And just at this point the Cairo codex becomes available; it gives us the next 350 lines virtually complete.

20 But, unlike Smikrines, the Euripidean arbitrator, Cercyon, recognized the objects that had been left with the baby as belonging to his daughter – and ordered his daughter to be put to death.

21 The formal debate (*agōn*) was a standard feature of Old Comedy, but in New Comedy it is rare. In Aristophanes an *agon* is always won by the

second speaker, so many spectators may realize from the start that Daos is destined to be the loser. It is noteworthy that while Daos' speech is interrupted four times (probably twice by Syriskos and twice by Smikrines), Syriskos' slightly longer speech (he has fifty-nine lines to Daos' fifty-three) is not interrupted at all.

22 This was a respectful form of address to an older person.

23 Sons of Poseidon and Tyro, who became kings of Pylos and Iolcus respectively. The most famous dramatization of the story was by Sophocles (in two plays called *Tyro*), though Syriskos' account seems rather muddled (how did the goatherd know the boys were of high birth, and how could tokens supplied by him be of any use for identification?)

24 No tragic example of this scenario is known, though something similar occurs (to the great chagrin of the brother, Moschion) in Menander's own *Perikeiromene*, and there are several myths that could have been 'tweaked' by a fourth-century dramatist to create such a story. In Sophocles' *Mysians* the story of Telephus is similarly tweaked so that Telephus narrowly avoids marrying his *mother*, though in this instance recognition tokens are not involved.

25 As in several plays of Euripides (*Antiope, Hypsipyle, Melanippe the Captive*) and one of Sophocles' *Tyro* plays, though in each case the mother is saved by *twin* sons, and only in *Hypsipyle* is the recognition effected through tokens.

26 For the saving of a brother, most critics refer to Euripides' *Iphigeneia in Tauris* (Orestes saved by Iphigeneia from human sacrifice), but there the recognition is not effected through tokens; possibly Syriskos is muddling this recognition with the earlier recognition of Orestes by his other sister Electra, which in at least two versions (in Aeschylus' *Libation Bearers* and Sophocles' *Electra*) did involve one or more tokens, but which did not so much 'save' Orestes as facilitate his taking of revenge for his father's murder.

27 It may be worth drawing attention to the fact (in which no commentator appears to take any interest) that this charcoal-burning slave is assumed to be literate enough to read an unfamiliar name engraved in what must be quite small lettering. Niall Slater points out that a signature, like a modern designer label, would probably enhance the value of the object – and therefore (I add) heighten Syriskos' suspicions of Onesimos' motive in demanding it.

28 On rape as a plot element in New Comedy, see Ch. 5.

29 This would be all the more incomprehensible to Habrotonon if Charisios had hired her, not simply as part of the entertainment for a series of daytime parties, but for twenty-four-hour attendance. And while the state of the text in Act I prevents absolute certainty, it is likely that we should indeed suppose the hiring to have been of that kind: (1) in the play's opening sentence Karion speaks of Charisios as 'having' (*ekhōn*) Habrotonon, a verb that in such contexts normally implies a settled relationship; (2) he is paying a high price for her services (136–8); (3) she came to the job expecting him to be in love with her (432). If so, she has been waiting in vain for his amorous attentions not only for two days and a bit, but for two whole nights as well.

30 Hardly by killing him; more likely by selling him to work in a mill or a mine, or to a foreigner. In fact it is already too late for such precautions, since Onesimos has told the story to Karion, but Charisios does not know this.

31 In ancient Greece, as in many other slave societies, a child was deemed to be a slave if its mother was a slave, regardless of the status of its father. Habrotonon's expectation is that Charisios will buy her from her owner and then set both her and the baby free. In fact things will take a different turn when she meets the baby's real mother; see p. 00 [61] n. 00 [56].

32 He has, in fact, conspicuously failed to match up to the role of that stock character of New Comedy, the scheming slave (Furley 2009a: 193).

33 'Realistically' we would expect to see some guests actually leaving Chairestratos' house at this point; but such a mass exodus (say, of four or five young men) would give undue prominence to a group of persons who are not dramatic characters at all (though they had been mentioned at 430–1 as having pestered Habrotonon), and probably their departure was left to the imagination, aided by Karion's words at 612.

34 So Sandbach's restoration of Smikrines' aside at 621, which is found plausible by all recent editors even though only the first two and the last four or five letters of the line survive.

35 He cannot make her his wife, even after divorcing Pamphile, since she is not a citizen.

36 Habrotonon is worth twelve drachmas a day to her owner (136–8); if she is hired only on half the days in the year, that makes an annual gross income stream of 2,160 drachmas or over one-third of a talent – and there are real-

life instances of skilled or attractive slaves being sold for four-figure sums (e.g. Xenophon, *Memorabilia* 2.5.2; [Demosthenes] 59.29). We are probably not meant to ask how Charisios was able to produce that kind of money when he had no access to his own coffers (which would be in his own home). Did he perhaps borrow it, on friendly (interest-free) terms (Millett 1992), from Chairestratos?

37 'He drank with Miss A, in the evening he had Miss B, and he was meaning to have Miss C tomorrow' (680–2).

38 On his legal right to do this, see Ch. 5, p. 51.

39 Literally 'unless we, the family he's married into, are resident aliens falsely registered (as citizens)'.

40 These last two utterances by Chairestratos – five Greek words altogether – are all he says between (at least) 679 and 697.

41 Bathrellou 2014b: 64–5 shows that Smikrines' last speech in Act III ends at 696.

42 See further Ch. 5, pp. 48–9, on the status of *nothoi* (bastards).

43 See Hunter 1985: 40–2; Ireland 1995: 16–17.

44 We will learn later that Charisios has been listening to this argument from behind Chairestratos' front door.

45 Literally 'you would no longer be judged to be a father but a master'.

46 Possibly the point is that she would not dare to eat, for fear that her husband might come home and be angry with her for not waiting for him; possibly it is that distress would take away her appetite.

47 Though it is striking that he apparently does not use what might have been his strongest argument, viz. the respect due to a parent; see the detailed analysis of his speech by Traill 2008: 179–88.

48 Small but important new fragments of the Michigan papyrus have been identified and published by Cornelia Römer (2012a, b, 2015, 2016); see also Casanova 2013, 2014b, c, Luppe 2013, Furley 2013, 2014a, 2016, Bathrellou 2014b, Furley 2021. The most recent of these have shown, among other things, that Smikrines expects that Habrotonon will use the methods of witchcraft (*pharmaka epiboula*, 787) to alienate Charisios' affections from Pamphile, and that Pamphile's speech begins two lines earlier than had previously been supposed (at 799, not 801) with an assurance that she would never do anything against her father's will (by the time her speech ends we may find this hard to believe, and so evidently did Smikrines).

49 She cannot of course breast-feed the baby, since she has not herself actually given birth. Presumably it is still getting its feeds from Syriskos' wife, who had a baby that died (268).

50 But Furley 2009a, citing a parallel from *Perikeiromene* 183, thinks the meaning is merely 'I'll get out of the way of this person who has come outside'.

51 It is amazing to the modern mind that the two women should both be overjoyed at the discovery that the stranger who had raped Pamphile less than a year ago is now her husband, and that this has made Pamphile, if anything, even more determined to stay with him; see Ch. 5.

52 Furley thinks he remains on stage, in some inconspicuous place; but how then could he later appeal for the support of Habrotonon (933–4) or even know where she was?

53 The Greek verb used here, *biazesthai*, can also mean 'rape', and the fact that Charisios, a rapist himself, can use it in another sense, with Pamphile as object, is further evidence that he does not fully appreciate the criminality of his conduct.

54 This was Sandbach's supplement (the Cairo codex has lost about seven letters at the beginning of the line); Furley proposes 'I thought it was mine' or 'So it's not mine, then?'

55 Thus in *Dyskolos*, the betrothal of Knemon's daughter to Sostratos is effected towards the end of Act IV; in Act V Sostratos secures the hand of his own sister for his new friend, Knemon's stepson Gorgias, and then various humbler characters attempt to persuade or coerce Knemon into taking part in the celebrations. In *Samia*, at the same stage, all obstacles to the marriage of Moschion and Plangon have been removed, but at the start of Act V a new if temporary obstacle is created by Moschion's resentment at being suspected by his adoptive father of having had an affair with the latter's *pallake* Chrysis. In these two plays the developments in Act V are unanticipated; in *Epitrepontes*, by contrast, we know that Chairestratos and Smikrines have gone on errands, and we expect them to return. In contrast with all these, as William Furley points out to me, the main issue of *Misoumenos* is not resolved until Act V.

56 She had expected to gain her freedom by persuading Charisios that she and he are the baby's parents (538–49); she did so persuade him, and he apparently took immediate steps to purchase her as a necessary

preliminary to setting her free. But now she has met and recognized Pamphile, Pamphile has been reunited with her son, and if Habrotonon does get her freedom, she will have got it not by duping Charisios into recognizing a bastard child, but by helping him to discover that he truly is the father of a legitimate one.

57 Rather similarly, in *Samia*, Moschion, having raped Plangon, made her pregnant, and immediately promised to marry her, finds at his eventual betrothal that he will receive no dowry – her father Nikeratos says he will give with his daughter 'all my property – when I die' (*Samia* 727–8), i.e. when the brotherless Plangon (or, in practice, her husband or her children) would have inherited it in any case. It will not be a large estate, either: Nikeratos is a poor man who has to do his own shopping, and who cannot afford to mend his leaky roof (*Samia* 592–3),

58 On *Auge* see further Collard and Cropp 2008: 259–77.

59 Today we would expect the mother to come as well, but Pamphile probably stayed at home with the baby – and maybe with Sophrone, who would be only too glad to be back with her old nursling.

Chapter 5

1 At Athens a wife could do this by notifying the *archon*. She would need to know that she had another home to go to, but for Pamphile this would present no difficulty.

2 Usually, as in *Epitrepontes*, the rape is said to have taken place at an all-night religious celebration, this being one of the few occasions when unmarried girls might be out of doors at night without male supervision; see Furley 2009b.

3 And, to multiply the injustice, if these material losses have any impact on the well-being of the husband/rapist, they will impact equally on the well-being of the wife/victim, who is totally dependent for her support on her dowry (if any) and her husband's resources and income.

4 A passage of the orator Lysias (1.32–3), often cited to show that rape was not so regarded, is grossly and deliberately misleading, comparing as it does the weakest of the possible sanctions against rape (a suit for damages) with the severest of the possible sanctions against adultery (summary

private execution of an offender caught in the act – which in any case
would be available whether the act was consensual or not). See Harris
2006: 283–95, Todd 2007: 126–34.

5   See e.g. Fisher 1992: 104–11; D. Cohen 1995: 153–4. The drafter of the law
against *hybris* must have had sexual offences at the front of his mind when
he specified its potential victims as 'a child, a woman or a man'
(Demosthenes 21.47; even if the text of the law cited there is a forgery, as
argued by Harris 2013: 224–31, the highly abnormal precedence given to
'woman' over 'man' – instinctively reversed in a quotation of the law by the
orator Aeschines (1.15) – can hardly be the forger's invention). The
argument of Omitowoju 2002 that a woman's consent was irrelevant to
Greek definitions of sexual crimes ignores much of the evidence (see
Sommerstein 2006).

6   As in the case of Themistius of Aphidna, who was executed for committing
hybris against 'the lyre-girl from Rhodes' during the festival of the Eleusinia
(Deinarchus 1.23); juries were not likely to be more lenient when the
victim was of citizen status.

7   Sostratos quickly satisfies Gorgias that he has none but honourable
intentions, and Gorgias is happy to become his ally in the seemingly
impossible task of persuading the girl's father (Gorgias' stepfather), the
misanthropic Knemon, to give her to Sostratos in marriage.

8   With this line of reasoning compare Harris 2006: 327–8, on attitudes in
Peru to the repeal in 1997 of a law which had given rapists immunity from
all punishment if they married their victims.

9   A parallel may be cited from Henry Fielding's eighteenth-century novel
Tom Jones. Bridget, the unmarried sister of Squire Allworthy, had become
pregnant by a young man named Summer, who soon afterwards died of
smallpox. In her sixth month, her brother opportunely went on a long visit
to London. Bridget then dismissed her maid and engaged Jenny Jones in
her place, and when her time came, she was delivered in the presence of
Jenny and her mother alone. On the day of Squire Allworthy's return, the
baby was put into his bed; Jenny was soon suspected of being its mother,
and 'confessed' at once. Bridget's son remained 'Tom Jones' for some twenty
years (his mother's deathbed confession having been suppressed by the
machinations of her younger, legitimate son) until Jenny (by then known
as Mrs Waters) revealed the truth.

10 On rape as a plot element in New Comedy, see further especially Rosivach 1998:13–50, also Lape 2001, Sommerstein 2013: 33–36, James 2014, Glazebrook 2015.

11 This rule was enacted on the proposal of Pericles in 451/0 BC; until then only the father had had to be a citizen, provided the mother was a free woman. On Athenian citizenship law see MacDowell 1978: 67–70, Todd 1993: 170–82, Patterson 2005: 278–89.

12 Girls as well as boys were presented in infancy to the members of their father's phratry: see Isaeus 3.73–9.

13 If he is brought up by the slave Syriskos and his wife, or if he is regarded as the child of the slave Habrotonon – and this is why Onesimos, and Habrotonon herself, expect that if Charisios believes that Habrotonon has a child of whom he is the father, he will buy her and set her free (538–49).

14 The case for this view was powerfully and convincingly argued by Ogden 1996: 151–65, and has not been seriously disputed since; for an earlier argument on the other side see e.g. MacDowell 1976.

15 For the object of adoption was not to provide a child with a home and parents, but to provide an heir for a family that lacked one – so that, for example, adoption was only possible for sons, not daughters; the adoptee had to have at least one brother who could be the heir of his natural father; and no one could adopt a son if he already had one.

16 *Eleutheros* 'free' is often used in comedy, in reference to women, to mean 'of citizen status' (and therefore, from a male citizen's point of view, 'marriageable'); cf. 495, *Dyskolos* 64, *Georgos* F 4.

17 It may be worth observing that it was only in 1959 that English law was amended so that a child born in these circumstances became legitimate if its parents afterwards married.

18 Brown was responding to an article by MacDowell (1982) who seemed to be taking the position that provisions of Athenian law could be directly deduced from comedy. This question, discussed by these scholars mainly with reference to *Aspis*, arises also in *Epitrepontes* over Smikrines' attempt to end his daughter's marriage. From what happens in the play we can reasonably infer that, at least under certain circumstances, an Athenian father had this right, and also that he might at the same time reclaim his daughter's dowry (cf. *Epitr*. 1079–80), but we cannot expect to learn any of the fine detail (e.g. whether the right lapsed when a child was born). In any

case, what matters dramatically about these scenes is not what Smikrines'
legal rights are, but such things as Pamphile's defiance, Charisios' reaction
to it, and the characterization of Smikrines as one who, if indeed he has
this legal right, 'is trying to exercise [it] without regard to the wishes or
feelings of members of his family' (Buis 2014: 336).

19 Which he would probably feel entitled to do; after all, the child's mother
would be of citizen status and *would* be his lawful wife (the words of
the oath said nothing about her having been his wife *at the time of the
child's birth*).

20 No case of exposure is mentioned in the entire corpus of lawcourt oratory.
At Gortyn in Crete, on the other hand, it was matter-of-factly referred to in
a legal text: 'if a divorced woman bears a child. she shall bring it to her
[ex-]husband at his house in the presence of three witnesses; and if he does
not accept it, the child shall be for the mother either to rear or to expose'
(*Inscriptiones Creticae* iv 72: III 44–9).

21 That this was a common practice, and taken for granted, is well illustrated
by a metaphorical reference to it in Aristophanes' *Clouds* (530–2).
Speaking, in the name of the poet, of his first play, *The Banqueters
(Daitalēs)*, which he had given to Callistratus to produce, in language
appropriate to a firstborn child, the chorus-leader says: 'Since I was
unmarried and not yet supposed to give birth, I exposed it, another girl
picked it up, and you [the Athenian theatre audience] generously reared
and educated it.' In New Comedy, nevertheless, mothers often avoid
exposing their children by asking a neighbour, a friend or even a stranger
to take charge of the child (Lape & Moreno 2014: 357–8); this is known to
have occurred in Menander's *Hiereia (The Priestess)* and *Phasma*.

22 Aristotle in his *Politics* (1335b19-23) has no qualms about recommending
that it should be forbidden by law to rear a severely disabled child, but
recognizes that 'settled custom' forbids the exposure of children merely on
account of their numbers (he nevertheless recommends a legal limit on
family size, with compulsory early abortion for those who break the limit).
On exposure due to poverty, it is noteworthy that in Menander's
Perikeiromene no one, including the children themselves, blames Pataikos
for exposing his son and daughter (twins) after his wife had died and his
ship, on which he relied for most of his income, had sunk in an Aegean
storm (*Perik.* 800–12). The Poseidippus fragment quoted in the next note

likewise implies that exposure was associated with poverty in the popular mind.

23 When Poseidippus, a dramatist of the generation after Menander, made a character say that 'every man rears a son, even if he's poor, but exposes a daughter even if he's rich' (fr. 12), he was of course exaggerating, but there must have been something to exaggerate.

24 If a girl was enslaved in this way, she was very likely to end up as a slave prostitute like Habrotonon.

25 'Almost' because occasionally it leads to disappointment for a particular character. In *Perikeiromene* Moschion has fallen in love with Glykera, and is none too pleased to discover she is his twin sister. (In the last surviving lines of the play, 1024–6, his father decides to arrange a marriage for him forthwith.)

26 This procedure, called *epidikasia*, applied only to 'heiresses' (*epiklēroi*), i.e. women whose father had died and who had no living brothers; they were required to marry the nearest relative who put in a claim, and if there was more than one claimant the *archon* (or, if his decision was challenged, the jury) had only to decide which was the closest relative, not which was the most suitable husband. See MacDowell 1978: 95–8, Schaps 1979: 25–47.

27 The only larger dowry attested at Athens by any half-credible source is that of ten talents allegedly given to Alcibiades by his very rich (and very extravagant) father-in-law Callias ([Andocides] 4.13). On Athenian dowries generally see Schaps 1979: 74–84, 99–105.

28 Even when one spouse died, if there were no children the dowry still had to be returned.

29 On the rules governing dissolution of marriage at Athens, see Cohn-Haft 1995.

30 More precisely, of the person who would be her *kyrios* if she were not married; this covers the case where, for example, the woman's father has died and his rights have passed to a brother or, if her brothers are all still children, to a relative appointed as their guardian.

31 Isaeus 3.78; Demosthenes 30.17, 26; [Andocides] 4.14; Plutarch, *Alcibiades* 8.3–5.

32 *Didot Papyrus* 1 = *Comica Adespota* fr. 1000: the wife's father wants to end the marriage because his son-in-law has fallen into poverty. It has been suggested that this passage may not be an excerpt from an actual comedy

but rather a student's exercise modelled on Pamphile's speech in *Epitrepontes* (Casanova 1997; Furley 2009a: 210; Casanova 2014c: 143). At Rome the theme appealed to dramatist and rhetorician alike (Plautus, *Stichus* 62–151; Ennius trag. 125–39 = *Rhetorica ad Herennium* 2.38; Seneca the Elder, *Controversiae* 2.2); see Traill 2008: 213–23, who points out that Pamphile's defiance of her father is more extreme and unequivocal than that of any of her counterparts, owing mainly (Traill argues) to her desperate need to conceal from him the fact that she is the mother of (as she believes) a bastard child. When assessing Charisios' reaction to her speech it is worth remembering that he *does* know this fact.

33 Contrast the alleged action of the much younger Alcibiades: when his wife was on her way to the *archon* to register her divorce, he and a posse of his friends seized her by force and took her home ([Andocides] 4.14).

34 Thus in *Samia* (381–2) Demeas, expelling Chrysis from his home for her supposed infidelity, affects to believe he is being generous in allowing her to keep 'maidservants and jewellery' (probably in point of fact one elderly servant and the jewellery she happens to be wearing at that moment).

35 Thus Neaera, a slave *hetaira* working in Corinth, was able to buy her freedom when her joint owners both decided to get married: having apparently bought her for 3,000 dr., they agreed to let her buy herself out of slavery for 2,000, and she was able to make up this sum from her own savings together with contributions from former lovers; her liberation was, however, conditional on her not working as a *hetaira* in Corinth (where her presence might be an embarrassment to her ex-owners).

36 He is paying twelve drachmae a day (136–8). In the 330s and 320s the charge for hiring a music-girl had been limited by law to two drachmae ([Aristotle], *Athenian Constitution* 50.2), an artificially low rate, as is evident from the fact that magistrates enforcing the law often had to draw lots among rival claimants for the same woman. This restriction probably disappeared at, or soon after, the fall of the classical democracy in 322, and a few years later, in *Samia* 392–6 (datable 320–314: Sommerstein 2013: 44–6) Chrysis is told that by hiring herself out for parties she can expect to make 'only' ten drachmae a time. Twelve a day is thus perhaps not an extravagant rate in itself (except in the eyes of the money-obsessed Smikrines), but it will mount up quickly if Charisios persists in this lifestyle.

37 Some of the other guests at Chairestratos' latest party eventually try to take advantage of his restraint by making passes at Habrotonon themselves (see 430–1, where she is apparently addressing these men).

Chapter 6

1 And of at least one person whom we never see, the anonymous slave-shepherd who felt it his duty to inform Syriskos that Daos was in possession of some trinkets which he had found with the baby.

2 So too at crucial points does one character's *misapprehension* of the personality (or indeed the identity) of another, from the trivial to the profound. Karion comes outside to vent his annoyance at the disruption of the lunch party by Habrotonon's accusation of Charisios, and finds there an old man who, unknown to him, is Charisios' already irate father-in-law. The marriage itself, we may be sure, would never have been made had Smikrines known that Charisios was the sort of man who would father, and then acknowledge, a bastard child. The importance of misapprehension in Menandrian plots is insisted on by Traill 2008, with particular reference to misapprehensions regarding women. It is striking that Habrotonon, who is misjudged more often and more drastically than anyone else in *Epitrepontes* (Traill 2008: 196–204), is consistently shrewd and accurate in her judgement of others.

3 In the surviving text we do not learn how he discovered it.

4 As Habrotonon shrewdly puts it (468–70): 'if he really is your master's son, and you let him be brought up as a slave, wouldn't you deserve to be put to death?' If that is Habrotonon's view, how much more strongly will Charisios feel the same way, should he discover the truth about the child!

5 On the cook as a stock character in comedy see Wilkins 2000.

6 Probably resulting from annoyance at the loss of a fee (another typical element in the profile of the comic cook).

7 On Menander's presentation of women characters in *Epitrepontes* and in other plays, see Traill 2008, especially 177–242, and Lape 2010, especially 69–76.

8 Unless a client gives her a 'tip' over and above the fee agreed with her owner. As Traill 2008: 204 points out, almost all the other characters, from

Smikrines to Onesimos, misjudge Habrotonon by applying to her one or more features of the conventional stereotype of a *hetaira*.

9 Another Menandrian *hetaira*, Chrysis in *Samia*, likewise strives for the safety and welfare of a baby not hers, even at the risk first of her home and later (*Samia* 556–70) of her very life.

10 Habrotonon is very fond of using the adjective *glukus* 'sweet' in addressing people of both sexes, and she makes extensive use of several other lexical items, notably *talan* 'poor thing' (434, 439, 466, 546, 853, 970), which in comedy are found exclusively, or almost exclusively, on the lips of women and, in Menander, specifically of *lower-class* women – the speech of Pamphile, from a wealthy citizen family, has none of these features. See Ferrari 2014: 161–5, 169–70 and, on 'characterization by language' in Menander generally, Sandbach 1970, Arnott 1995.

11 The relationship could become permanent only if Chairestratos renounced all prospect of marriage, or if Habrotonon were discovered to be of citizen birth and so eligible to marry him. Both these scenarios are contrary to the ground rules of New Comedy: decent young men are expected to marry, and a citizen woman entering her first marriage, even if brought up among *hetairai* (e.g. after being captured by pirates), must not have been carnally known by any man except her bridegroom. The partner of a *hetaira* might, however, on terminating the relationship, make her a parting gift which could enable her (if a slave) to buy her freedom or (if already free) to live independently without having to practise her former trade; compare e.g. [Demosthenes] 59.30–32.

12 As often in Menander, 'the surface-level plot of mistaken identity is only the catalyst to the real drama of revealed character' (Furley 2014b: 108).

13 In fact, though, when Smikrines comes back 'for his dowry and his daughter', it is not Charisios who confronts him but Onesimos (and later Chairestratos).

14 From the surviving text it is not clear whether Sophrone is still a slave or whether, like another ex-nurse in *Samia* (236–8; cf. [Demosthenes] 47.55–6), she had been given her freedom. It may be significant that Smikrines' threats to drown her if she contradicts him again (1070–5) succeed in silencing her – though even as a freedwoman, one feels, Sophrone would not have been wise to rely on her legal right not to be murdered.

15 As Lamagna 2014:105 puts it, with reference to Menandrian comedy in general: 'one feels a sensation of delicacy combined with inevitability, in which every piece is in its right place as if in a solved jigsaw puzzle where no one would ever think of the possibility of an alternative solution.'

Chapter 7

1 Assuming that Sophrone is no longer a slave (see Ch. 6 n. 14).

2 On Smikrines' role, see Austin 2011.

3 Here, and again at the end of Act III, Smikrines enters Charisios' house without the consent of the owner; but nobody criticizes him specifically for this reason, and we may assume that this action was considered permissible because Charisios had left home without any indication of when, or even whether, he was returning, Pamphile had been left alone, and her father was her natural protector.

4 He could then, if necessary, sue Charisios for the return of the dowry, with interest at 18 per cent (which, on a sum of four talents, would amount to 360 drachmae per month).

5 Believing his nephew Kleostratos to have been killed while campaigning abroad, leaving a sister who thereby becomes an *epikleros* (see p. 00 [40]), Smikrines insists on claiming her hand, regardless of the views, interests and feelings of every other member of his family – for, as a goddess says in the prologue (116–18), he 'utterly surpasses all men in wickedness; he knows neither kinsman nor friend'. The family set out to frustrate him by faking the death of his brother (whose daughter would then also become an *epikleros*, with a much larger inheritance), but before their plot can reach its climax Kleostratos comes home alive and well.

6 And even she is told in effect, at great length, that she is a fool to want to stay with her husband; and we cannot tell how cutting Smikrines' language to her may have been in the large portion of his speech which has not survived, or in parting words just before he left to fetch Sophrone.

7 One would expect that, as the daughter of a rich man, Pamphile would have been given a maidservant or two at her marriage, but there is no mention of this in the text we have. Perhaps this is an accident of preservation, or perhaps Menander wished to stress her isolation. Ideally a

household should never be without an adult male head, though of course many actual households failed to match this ideal.

8 She knows that she would be worse than out of place at the moment of Charisios' reunion with his wife, and she will by now be well aware of Chairestratos' interest in her. He is out of the house at present, but will certainly be returning soon.

9 Of which, so far as we can tell, only he is aware, since Syriskos never explains to Onesimos how he came by the baby and the jewellery.

10 At a point which, by a curious coincidence, now bears the line-number 908.

11 Which, having been brought from Delphi to Phthia for this purpose, is then on the instructions of Thetis taken straight back to Delphi and buried there.

12 But Menander has another, negative surprise in store. With Charisios back in his own house, and Smikrines intending to make another attempt to take Pamphile away, we expect a climactic confrontation between them, and in 927–31 Charisios himself anticipates this and imagines what he will say. It never happens; instead Smikrines is confronted, and humiliated, by Onesimos.

Chapter 8

1 But not the very earliest. Sophocles too had written an *Andromeda* (datable c. 450), and his *Oenomaus* (datable 445–20) had presented the love story of Pelops and Hippodameia. See Klimek-Winter 1993: 23–54 and Talboy & Sommerstein 2012, also Sommerstein 2020.

2 Examples of 'worse' characters would be Thoas in *Iphigeneia in Tauris* and Theoclymenus in *Helen* – though both of these suffer nothing worse than the humiliating frustration of a nefarious scheme (resembling in this respect a Menandrian villain like the Smikrines of *Aspis*).

3 On Menander's debts to tragedy, especially Euripides, see Katsouris 1975, Hunter 1985: 114–36, Hurst 1990, Gutzwiller 2000, Cusset 2003, Martina 2016: iii 11–266; on *Epitrepontes* in particular, Anderson 1982, Porter 2000, Furley 2009a: 2–8.

4 On the mythical and tragic references and allusions in this passage, see p. 107 nn. 24–6.

5 Who was drunk (Euripides fr. 272b).

6 In all probability Heracles, like Charisios, had left the ring inadvertently, perhaps having it torn off his finger in a struggle.

7 On *Alope* see further Collard and Cropp 2008: 113–23.

8 Literally 'to be shut in for death', i.e. to be imprisoned or walled up without food.

9 He thus has no opportunity to threaten the lives of his daughter and grandson, as Cercyon does with fatal consequences for Alope – although he does threaten to murder Sophrone, not for concealing the child's birth (for he still does not know of this) but for daring to criticize her (?former) master (1062–75). Murderous rage against one's own offspring was not necessarily alien to comedy: Nikeratos in *Samia* (553–86), on discovering that his daughter has given birth out of wedlock, is ready to kill the baby, his own wife, and the lady next door who helped conceal the birth – but he proves a thoroughly incompetent murderer.

10 On Aristotelian ideas in *Epitrepontes* and in Menander generally, see Fortenbaugh 1974, Casanova 2014c, Cinaglia 2014, Konstan 2014: 290–2.

11 In Scotland called 'culpable homicide'; in many jurisdictions one of the most common varieties of unintentional but blameworthy killing is treated as a separate offence of 'causing death by dangerous driving' or the like.

12 Outside the United States there are often no degrees of murder, but a comparable distinction is usually still made at the sentencing stage.

13 The master, Moschion, had himself used the milder term *hamartanein* (*Samia* 3).

14 Forgiveness, to be sure, is highly valued in Menander's ethical world, but even by his standards Pamphile is at the extreme end of the spectrum, since Charisios has neither sought forgiveness nor given any indication that he recognizes he has done wrong. Indeed, whereas normally in Menander forgiveness comes in answer to repentance, here repentance comes in answer to forgiveness. See Gutzwiller 2012, especially 72–4. Pamphile's exceptional magnanimity wins an exceptional reward when, a few minutes later, she is not only reunited with her baby but learns that it is legitimate and also that her husband's supposed affair with Habrotonon had never happened.

Chapter 9

1 Though his record of eight first prizes in about thirty years (at Dionysia and Lenaea combined) is broadly comparable to that of Euripides, who won five Dionysian victories (one of them posthumous) in a career of fifty years.

2 A play of which not a word survives.

3 New Comedy also penetrated the thought-world of the educated citizen of the Roman empire, especially its Greek-speaking eastern half, in many other ways; see Marshall & Hawkins 2016.

4 *Bacchides, Cistellaria* and *Stichus.* In one section of *Bacchides* (494–562) we can see the precise nature and extent of Plautus' adaptation, thanks to a papyrus fragment of its source, Menander's *Dis Exapaton (The Double Deception).*

5 *Andria (The Woman from Andros), Heauton Timorumenos (The Man who Punished Himself), Eunuchus (The Eunuch)* and *Adelphoe (The Brothers).*

6 In the Mertens-Pack[3] database of literary papyri (http://cipl93.philo.ulg. ac.be/Cedopal/MP3/dbsearch_en.aspx; accessed 15 April 2020), Homer has no fewer than 1,683 entries. Next among poets is Euripides (169), then Hesiod (137) and Menander (104) – but there are also many fragments which are clearly New Comedy but cannot be proved to be by Menander, though a large proportion are probably his. For comparison, there are fifty-nine entries for Aristophanes, fifty-five for Pindar, and only thirty-seven for Sophocles.

7 Fourteen, one of which (*Berlin Papyrus* 21142) is doubtfully attributed.

8 Alluding to the fact that Claudius had been considered a person of no account until he was unexpectedly made emperor after the assassination of his nephew Gaius in AD 41, when he was the only living adult male member of the Julio-Claudian family.

9 Among the twenty or so plays of Menander (a maximum figure) of which we know enough to pronounce on the matter with fair confidence, three feature as part of their back-story a rape committed by a character named Moschion: *Samia, Kitharistes (The Lyre Player),* and the *Fabula Incerta* of the Cairo codex.

10 In the case of Aeschylus, Sophocles and Aristophanes the select plays alone (seven, seven and eleven plays respectively) survived intact into the Middle

Ages. In the case of Euripides the ten select plays were supplemented by nine which survived from what had once been a complete corpus arranged alphabetically.

11 One of these, 'You must learn your letters and, having learned them, you must behave sensibly', was chosen as the epigraph of the Joint Association of Classical Teachers' textbook for those learning Greek for the first time, *Reading Greek*, where it is absurdly attributed to Menander.

12 The erasure is never perfect, and part at least of the underlying text can normally be read; such a document is known as a palimpsest.

13 The twenty-two lines are those now known as *Epitr.* 127–48. The lines on the other side of the leaf, first read by Uspensky, are now *Epitr.* 159–77. The numbering of verses now usual in *Epitrepontes*, as in some other Menandrian plays, was devised by A. W. Gomme with a view to leaving room for material yet to be discovered; inevitably the size of gaps usually cannot be determined with great precision, even when (as in this case) the gap is between passages in corresponding positions on consecutive pages, but the evidence of a more recent papyrus discovery (*Oxyrhynchus Papyrus* 4021, published in 1994) has shown that Gomme's estimate of a ten-line gap is at least close to the truth.

14 It is instructive to compare the fate of Jernstedt's publication with that of a book by a colleague of his at St Petersburg that was published in German a few years earlier: the monograph by the Polish scholar Tadeusz Zieliński (1885) on the structural divisions of Old Comedy (*Die Gliederung der altattischen Komödie*), which quickly and deservedly came to be regarded as the fundamental work on its subject.

15 Of these fragments themselves, by the way, little was heard for many years, and they were widely believed to have disappeared in one or another of the upheavals that had befallen Russia. In fact they had all along been in the same library (later called the Saltykov-Shchedrin State Public Library; now the National Library of Russia) in St Petersburg, subsequently Petrograd, subsequently Leningrad, now again St Petersburg (see www.nlr.ru/eng/coll/manuscripts/greek.html).

16 It is all but certain that the manuscript once contained other plays too, which have been lost completely.

17 Sometimes 'the unidentified Cairo play' (*fabula incerta Cairensis*). In Arnott's Loeb Classical Library edition (Arnott 1979–2000: iii 426–72) it is

Fabula Incerta 1. Arnott prints four additional fragments from other papyri, which might or might not come from the same play; if they all do, it would bring the total number of lines wholly or partly preserved to about 186 – and it would still be impossible to identify the play.

18 This personal name is not found in any comic text or fragment other than *Epitrepontes*, unless *Berlin Papyrus* 21142 comes from a different play.

19 This would be impossible under the conventions of the genre; see Ch. 5 p. 00 [29].

20 See apgrd.ox.ac.uk/research-collections/performance-database/ productions (accessed 4 August 2020).

21 We have seen in Ch. 5 that the tendency to take a forgiving attitude to rape was an inevitable one, given certain other features of the contemporary culture; but the justified reaction to this of most moderns will be 'so much the worse for the contemporary culture'.

22 And if, as seems most likely, the final celebratory feast was held in Chairestratos' house, Charisios would almost certainly have attended it without his wife, who could not have been invited by a young man who was not a relation, nor dine in the company of a *hetaira*, even if that *hetaira* had been the saviour of her child.

23 A little earlier than in Menander's original (before the Pamphile-Habrotonon recognition scene), to make it immediately clear to the audience that he has been eavesdropping on the argument between Pamphile and Smikrines.

24 Though this is not without parallel in Menander: in *Samia* (67–9) Parmenon reminds his master Moschion of the duty he owes to 'the girl you wronged, and her mother', and calls him 'you womanish creature' (*androgyne*).

References

Akrigg B. and Tordoff R. L. eds. 2013. *Slaves and Slavery in Ancient Greek Comic Drama.* Cambridge: Cambridge University Press.

Alston R., Hall E. M. and Proffitt L. eds. 2011. *Reading Ancient Slavery.* London: Bristol Classical Press.

Anderson W. S. 1982. Euripides' *Auge* and Menander's *Epitrepontes. Greek, Roman and Byzantine Studies* 23: 165–77.

Apostolakis K. 2019. *Timokles: Translation and Commentary.* Göttingen: Vandenhoeck and Ruprecht.

Arnott W. G. 1979–2000. *Menander* (3 vols) Cambridge, MA: Harvard University Press.

Arnott W. G. 1987. The Time-scale of Menander's *Epitrepontes. Zeitschrift für Papyrologie und Epigraphik* 70: 19–31.

Arnott W. G. 1995. Menander's Manipulation of Language for the Individualisation of Character. In De Martino and Sommerstein 1995: ii 147–64.

Arnott W. G. 1996. *Alexis: The Fragments.* Cambridge: Cambridge University Press.

Arnott W. G. 1999. The Length of Menander's *Samia. Zeitschrift für Papyrologie und Epigraphik* 128: 45–48.

Austin C. F. L. 2011. 'My daughter and her dowry': Smikrines in Menander's *Epitrepontes.* In Obbink and Rutherford 2011: 160–73.

Balme D. M. and Brown P. G. McC. 2001. *Menander: The Plays and Fragments.* Oxford: Oxford University Press.

Bathrellou E. 2012. Menander's *Epitrepontes* and the Festival of the Tauropolia. *Classical Antiquity* 31: 151–92.

Bathrellou E. 2014a. Relationships among Slaves in Menander. In Sommerstein 2014: 40–57.

Bathrellou E. 2014b. On Menander, Epitrepontes 693–701 and 786–823. ZPE 192: 63–84.

Bayliss A. J. 2011. *After Demosthenes: The Politics of Early Hellenistic Athens.* London: Bloomsbury.

Blanchard A. 1997. Destins de Ménandre. *Ktèma* 22: 213–25; revised in Blanchard 2007: 9–27.

Blanchard A. 2007. *La comédie de Ménandre: politique, éthique, esthétique.* Paris: Presses de l'Université de Paris-Sorbonne.

Blanchard A. 2013. *Ménandre, Tome II: Le Héros, L'Arbitrage, La Tondue, La Fabula Incerta du Caire*. Paris: Les Belles Lettres.

Blundell J. 1980. *Menander and the Monologue*. Göttingen: Vandenhoeck and Ruprecht.

Brown P. G. McC. 1983. Menander's Dramatic Technique and the Law of Athens. *Classical Quarterly* n.s. 33: 412–20.

Brown P. G. McC. 1993. Love and Marriage in Greek New Comedy. *Classical Quarterly* n.s. 43: 289–305; reprinted in Segal 2001: 53–64.

Buis E. J. 2014. Law and Greek Comedy. In Fontaine and Scafuro 2014: 321–39.

Cairns D. L. and Liapis V. 2006. *Dionysalexandros: Essays on Aeschylus and his Fellow Tragedians in Honour of Alexander F. Garvie*. Swansea: Classical Press of Wales.

Canevaro M. 2013. *The Documents in the Attic Orators: Laws and Decrees in the Public Speeches of the Demosthenic Corpus*. Oxford: Oxford University Press.

Casanova A. 2013. Sui nuovi frammenti dell'atto IV degli 'Epitrepontes': note sulla 'rhesis' di Panfile. *Zeitschrift für Papyrologie und Epigraphik* 186: 94–9.

Casanova A. ed. 2014a. *Menandro e l'evoluzione della commedia greca: atti del convegno internazionale di studi in memoria di Adelmo Barigazzi*. Florence: Firenze University Press.

Casanova A. 2014b. Adelmo Barigazzi e il discorso di Panfile. In Casanova 2014a: 9–23.

Casanova A. 2014c. Menander and the Peripatos: New Insights into an Old Question. In Sommerstein 2014: 137–51.

Cinaglia V. 2014. Menander, Aristotle, Chance and Accidental Ignorance. In Sommerstein 2014: 152–66.

Cobet C. G. 1876. Menandri fragmenta inedita. *Mnemosyne* n.s. 4: 285–93.

Cohen D. 1995. *Law, Violence, and Community in Classical Athens*. Cambridge: Cambridge University Press.

Cohen E. E. 2015. *Athenian Prostitution: The Business of Sex*. Oxford: Oxford University Press.

Collard C. and Cropp M. J. 2008. *Euripides VII: Fragments, Aegeus-Meleager*. Cambridge, MA: Harvard University Press.

Cousland J. R. C. and Hume J. R. eds. 2009. *The Play of Texts and Fragments: Essays in Honour of Martin Cropp*. Leiden: Brill.

Csapo E. G. 1999. Performance and Iconographic Tradition in the Illustrations of Menander. *Syllecta Classica* 10: 154–88.

Csapo E. G. 2010. The Production and Performance of Comedy in Antiquity. In Dobrov 2010: 103–42.

Csapo E. G. et al. eds. 2014. *Greek Theatre in the Fourth Century B. C.* Berlin: De Gruyter.

Davidson J. N. 1997. *Courtesans and Fishcakes: The Consuming Passions of Classical Athens.* London: HarperCollins.

De Martino F. and Sommerstein A. H. eds. 1995. *Lo spettacolo delle voci.* Bari: Levante Editori.

Dobrov G. W. ed. 2010. *Brill's Companion to the Study of Greek Comedy.* Leiden: Brill.

Easterling P. E. 1995. Menander: Loss and Survival. In Griffiths 1995: 155–60.

Edmonds J. M. 1961. *The Fragments of Attic Comedy, after Meineke, Bergk, and Kock, Augmented, Newly Edited with their Contexts, Annotated, and Completely Translated into English Verse. Vol. IIIB: Menander.* Leiden: Brill.

Faraone C. A. and McClure L. K. eds. 2006. *Prostitutes and Courtesans in the Ancient World.* Madison: University of Wisconsin Press.

Ferrari F. 2014. Nell'officina di Menandro: idioletto femminile e marginalità sociale. In Casanova 2014a: 59–171.

Finglass P. J. and Coo L. 2020. *Female Characters in Fragmentary Greek Tragedy.* Cambridge: Cambridge University Press.

Fisher N. R. E. 1992. *Hybris: A Study in the Values of Honour and Shame in Ancient Greece.* Warminster: Aris and Phillips.

Fontaine M. and Scafuro A. C. eds. 2014. *The Oxford Handbook of Greek and Roman Comedy.* Oxford: Oxford University Press.

Fortenbaugh W. W. 1974. Menander's *Perikeiromene*: Misfortune, Vehemence, and Polemon. Phoenix 28: 430–43.

Furley W. D. 2009a. *Menander: Epitrepontes.* London: Institute of Classical Studies.

Furley W. D. 2009b. Drama at the Festival: A Recurrent Motif in Menander. In Cousland and Hume 2009: 389–401.

Furley W. D. 2014a. *Revisiting* Some Questions in the Text of *Epitrepontes.* In Casanova 2014a: 25–39.

Furley W. D. 2014b. Aspects of Recognition in *Perikeiromene* and Other Plays. In Sommerstein 2014: 106–15.

Furley W. D. 2016. More New Fragments of Menander's *Epitrepontes*: C. Römer, *ZPE* 196 (2015) 49–54. *Zeitschrift für Papyrologie und Epigraphik* 198: 19–21.

Furley W.D. 2021. New Fragments of Menander's Epitrepontes. London: University of London Press (open access publication at https://humanities-digital-library.org/index.php/hdl/catalog/book/new-fragments-menander.

Glazebrook A. 2015. A Hierarchy of Violence? Sex Slaves, *Parthenoi*, and Rape in Menander's *Epitrepontes*. *Helios* 42: 81–101.

Goldberg S. M. 1980. *The Making of Menander's Comedy.* Berkeley: University of California Press.

Gomme A. W. and Sandbach F. H. 1973. *Menander: A Commentary.* Oxford: Oxford University Press.

Green J. R. 2010. The Material Evidence. In Dobrov 2010: 71–102.

Griffiths A. H. ed. 1995. *Stage Directions: Essays in Ancient Drama in Honour of E. W. Handley.* London: Institute of Classical Studies.

Griswold C. L. and Konstan D. eds. 2012. *Ancient Forgiveness: Classical, Judaic, and Christian.* Cambridge: Cambridge University Press.

Gutzwiller K. J. 2000. The Tragic Mask of Comedy: Metatheatricality in Menander. *Classical Antiquity* 19: 102–37.

Gutzwiller K. J. 2012. All in the Family: Forgiveness and Reconciliation in New Comedy. In Griswold and Konstan 2012: 48–75.

Habicht C. 1997. *Athens from Alexander to Antony* (trans. D. L. Schneider). Cambridge MA: Harvard University Press.

Handley E. W. 2011. The Date of Menander's *Epitrepontes. Zeitschrift für Papyrologie und Epigraphik* 178: 51–3.

Handley E. W. and Hurst A. eds. 1990. *Relire Ménandre.* Geneva: Droz.

Harris E. M. 2006. *Democracy and the Rule of Law in Classical Athens: Essays in Law, Society, and Politics.* Cambridge: Cambridge University Press.

Harris E. M. 2013. The *Against Meidias* (Dem. 21). In Canevaro 2013: 209–36.

Harrison G. W. M. and Liapis V. J. eds. 2013 *Performance in Greek and Roman Theatre.* Leiden: Brill.

Heap A. 2002/3. The Baby as Hero? The Role of the Infant in Menander. *Bulletin of the Institute of Classical Studies* 46: 77–129.

Henderson T. R. 2020. *The Springtime of the People: The Athenian Ephebeia and Citizen Training from Lykourgos to Augustus.* Leiden: Brill.

Hunter R. L. 1985. *The New Comedy of Greece and Rome.* Cambridge: Cambridge University Press.

Hurst A. 1990. Ménandre et la tragédie. In Handley and Hurst 1990: 93–122.

Ireland S. 1995. *Menander: The Bad-Tempered Man (Δύσκολος).* Warminster: Aris and Phillips.

Ireland S. 2010a. *Menander: The Shield (Aspis) and The Arbitration (Epitrepontes).* Oxford: Aris and Phillips.

Ireland S. 2010b. New Comedy. In Dobrov 2010: 333–96.

Ireland S. 2019a. Gods (in New Comic Prologues). In Sommerstein 2019: 3
92–3.

Ireland S. 2019b. Prologue, Divine. In Sommerstein 2019: 775–6.

Iversen P. A. 2011. Menander's *Thaïs*: 'hac primum iuvenum lascivos lusit
amores'. *Classical Quarterly* n.s. 61: 186–91.

Jaekel S. 1964. *Menandri Sententiae; Comparatio Menandri et Philistionis*.
Leipzig: Teubner.

James S. L. 2014. Reconsidering Rape in Menander's Comedy and Athenian
Life: Modern Comparative Evidence. In Sommerstein 2014: 24–39.

Jernstedt V. 1891. *Porfirievskie otryvki iz attičeskoi komedii: paleografičeskie i
filologičeskie etjudy [Bishop Porphyry's Fragments of Attic Comedy:
Palaeographical and Philological Studies]*. St Petersburg: Historical-
Philosophical Faculty, Imperial University of St Petersburg.

Katsouris A. G. 1975. *Tragic Patterns in Menander*. Athens: Hellenic Society for
Humanistic Studies.

Kiritsi S. 2014. Menander's *Epitrepontes* in Modern Greek Theatre: The
Poetics of its Reception and Performance. In Sommerstein 2014:
231–48.

Kiritsi S. 2019. Evstratiades, Evstratios. In Sommerstein 2019: 344–5.

Klimek-Winter R. 1993. *Andromedatragödien: Sophokles, Euripides, Livius
Andronikos, Ennius, Accius*. Stuttgart: Teubner.

Konstan D. 2013. Menander's Slaves: The Banality of Violence. In Akrigg
and Tordoff 2013: 144–58.

Konstan D. 2014. Crossing Conceptual Worlds: Greek Comedy and
Philosophy. In Fontaine and Scafuro 2014: 278–94.

Konstantakos J. M. 2008. *Rara coronato plausere theatra Menandro?*
Menander's Success in his Lifetime. *Quaderni Urbinati di Cultura Classica*
n.s. 88: 79–106.

Lamagna M. 2014. La bottega dell'orologiaio: scene a tre personaggi in
Menandro. In Casanova 2014a: 105–20.

Lape S. 2001. Democratic Ideology and the Poetics of Rape in Menandrian
Comedy. *Classical Antiquity* 20: 79–119.

Lape S. and Moreno A. 2014. Comedy and the Social Historian. In Revermann
2014: 336–69.

Lefebvre G. 1907. *Fragments d'un manuscrit de Ménandre*. Cairo: Institut
Français d'Archéologie Orientale.

Luppe W. 2013. Zum Schluß des neuen Ἐπιτρέποντες-Fragments. *Zeitschrift
für Papyrologie und Epigraphik* 184: 102.

MacDowell D. M. 1976. Bastards as Athenian Citizens. *Classical Quarterly* n.s. 26: 88–91.

MacDowell D. M. 1978. *The Law in Classical Athens*. London: Thames and Hudson.

MacDowell D. M. 1982. Love Versus the Law: An Essay on Menander's *Aspis*. *Greece and Rome* 29: 42–52.

Manieri A. 2019a. Mouseia. In Sommerstein 2019: 575–6.

Manieri A. 2019b. Thespiae. In Sommerstein 2019: 949.

Marshall C. W. 2013. Sex Slaves in New Comedy. In Akrigg and Tordoff 2013: 173–96.

Marshall C. W. and Hawkins T. eds. 2016. *Athenian Comedy in the Roman Empire*. London: Bloomsbury.

Martina A. 2000. *Menandro: Epitrepontes II.1 (Prolegomeni), II.2 (Commento)*. Rome: Kepos.

Martina A. 2016. *Menandrea: elementi e struttura della commedia di Menandro* (3 vols). Pisa: Fabrizio Serra.

Millett P. C. 1992. *Lending and Borrowing in Ancient Athens*. Cambridge: Cambridge University Press.

Murray G. G. A. 1942. *The Rape of the Locks: The Perikeiromenê of Menander*, the fragments translated and the gaps conjecturally filled. London: Allen and Unwin.

Murray G. G. A. 1945. *The Arbitration: The Epitrepontes of Menander, Translated and Completed*. London: Allen and Unwin.

Nervegna S. 2013. *Menander in Antiquity: The Contexts of Reception*. Cambridge: Cambridge University Press.

Obbink D. and Rutherford R. B. eds. 2011. *Culture in Pieces: Essays on Ancient Texts in Honour of Peter Parsons*. Oxford: Oxford University Press.

Ogden D. 1996. *Greek Bastardy in the Classical and Hellenistic Periods*. Oxford: Oxford University Press.

Omitowoju R. 2002. *Rape and the Politics of Consent in Classical Athens*. Cambridge: Cambridge University Press.

Papastamati-von Moock Ch. 2014. The Theatre of Dionysus Eleuthereus in Athens: New Data and Observations on its 'Lycurgan' Phase. In Csapo et al. 2014: 15–76.

Patterson C. B. 2005. Athenian Citizenship Law. In Gagarin and Cohen 2005: 267–89.

Pernigotti C. 2008. *Menandri Sententiae*. Florence: Olschki.

Porter J. R. 2000. Euripides and Menander: *Epitrepontes*, Act IV. *Illinois Classical Studies* 24/25: 157–73.

Potter D. S. 1987. Telesphoros, Cousin of Demetrius: A Note on the Trial of Menander. *Historia* 36: 491–5.

Proffitt L. 2011. Family, Slavery and Subversion in Menander's *Epitrepontes*. In Alston et al. 2011: 152–74.

Revermann M. ed. 2014. *The Cambridge Companion to Greek Comedy*. Cambridge: Cambridge University Press.

Römer C. 2012a. New Fragments of Act IV, Epitrepontes 786–823 Sandbach (PMich 4752 a, b and c). *Zeitschrift für Papyrologie und Epigraphik* 182: 112–20.

Römer C. 2012b. A New Fragment of End of Act III, Epitrepontes 690–701 Sandbach (PMich 4805). *Zeitschrift für Papyrologie und Epigraphik* 183: 33–6.

Römer C. 2015. News from Smikrines and Pamphile: Two New Fragments of *Epitrepontes* 786–803 and 812–820 Sandbach-Furley. *Zeitschrift für Papyrologie und Epigraphik* 196: 49–54.

Römer C. 2016. News from Smikrines and Chairestratos: Verses 645–660 of 'Epitrepontes' Sandbach-Furley. *Zeitschrift für Papyrologie und Epigraphik* 197: 38–41.

Rosivach V. J. 1998. *When a Young Man Falls in Love: The Sexual Exploitation of Women in New Comedy*. London: Routledge.

Roueché C. 1993. *Performers and Partisans at Aphrodisias in the Roman and Late Roman Periods: A Study Based on Inscriptions from the Current Excavations at Aphrodisias in Caria*. London: Society for the Promotion of Roman Studies.

Ruffell I. A. 2014. Character Types. In Revermann 2014: 147–67.

Sandbach F. H. 1970. Menander's Manipulation of Language for Dramatic Purposes. In Turner 1970: 113–36.

Sandbach F. H. 1972. *Menandri reliquiae selectae*. Oxford: Clarendon Press.

Sandbach F. H. 1990. *Menandri reliquiae selectae*. 2nd edn, Oxford: Clarendon Press.

Scafuro A. C 2014a. Comedy in the Late Fourth and Early Third Centuries BCE. In Fontaine and Scafuro 2014: 199–217.

Scafuro A. C. 2014b. Menander. In Fontaine and Scafuro 2014: 218–38.

Schaps D. M. 1979. *Economic Rights of Women in Ancient Greece*. Edinburgh: Edinburgh University Press.

Segal E. ed. 2001. *Oxford Readings in Menander, Plautus, and Terence*. Oxford: Oxford University Press.

Slater N. W. 1996. Bringing up Father: *paideia* and *ephebeia* in the *Wasps*. In Sommerstein and Atherton 1996: 27–52.

Sommerstein A. H. 1990. *The Comedies of Aristophanes, Vol. 7: Lysistrata*. Warminster: Aris and Phillips.

Sommerstein A. H. 1996. Response to Slater 1996. In Sommerstein and Atherton 1996: 53–65. Reprinted with updates in Sommerstein 2009: 192–203.

Sommerstein A. H. 2006. Rape and Consent in Athenian Tragedy. In Cairns and Liapis 2006: 233–51.

Sommerstein A. H. 2008. *Aeschylus* (3 vols) Cambridge MA: Harvard University Press.

Sommerstein A. H. 2009. *Talking about Laughter and Other Studies in Greek Comedy*. Oxford: Oxford University Press.

Sommerstein A. H. 2013. *Menander: Samia (The Woman from Samos}*. Cambridge: Cambridge University Press.

Sommerstein A. H. ed. 2014. *Menander in Contexts*. New York: Oxford University Press.

Sommerstein A. H. ed. 2019. *The Encyclopedia of Greek Comedy* (3 vols, continuously paginated). Hoboken NJ: Wiley-Blackwell.

Sommerstein A. H. 2020. Women in Love in the Fragmentary Plays of Sophocles. In Finglass and Coo 2020: 62–72.

Sommerstein A. H. and Atherton C. eds. 1996. *Education in Greek Fiction*. Bari: Levante.

Sommerstein A. H. and Talboy T. H. 2012. *Sophocles: Selected Fragmentary Plays II*. Oxford: Aris and Phillips.

Talboy T. H. and Sommerstein A. H. 2012. *Oenomaus*. In Sommerstein and Talboy 2012: 75–109.

Todd S. C. 1993. *The Shape of Athenian Law*. Oxford: Clarendon Press.

Todd S. C. 2007. *A Commentary on Lysias, Speeches 1–11*. Oxford: Oxford University Press.

Tordoff R. L. 2013. Actors' Properties in Ancient Greek Drama: An Overview. In Harrison and Liapis 2013: 89–110.

Traill A. E. 2008. *Women and the Comic Plot in Menander*. Cambridge: Cambridge University Press.

Tribulato O. 2014. 'Not even Menander would use this word!' Perceptions of Menander's Language in Greek Lexicography. In Sommerstein 2014: 199–214.

Turner E. G. ed. 1970. *Ménandre: sept exposés suivis de discussions*. Geneva: Fondation Hardt.

Turner E. G. 1979. Menander and the New Society. *Chronique d'Égypte* 54: 106–12.

Vester C. 2013. Tokens of Identity in Menander's *Epitrepontes*: Slaves, Citizens and In-betweens. In Akrigg and Tordoff 2013: 209–27.

Webster T. B. L. 1974. *An Introduction to Menander*. Manchester: Manchester University Press.

Webster T. B. L., Green J. R. and Seeberg A. 1995. *Monuments Illustrating New Comedy*. 3rd ed. London: Institute of Classical Studies.

Wilamowitz-Moellendorff U. von 1925. *Menander: Das Schiedsgericht*. Berlin: Weidmann.

Wilkins J. M. 2000. *The Boastful Chef: The Discourse of Food in Ancient Greek Comedy*. Oxford: Oxford University Press.

Witzke S. S. 2019. Comedy, Modern Western. In Sommerstein 2019: 210–12.

Zagagi N. 1994. *The Comedy of Menander: Convention, Variation and Originality*. Bloomington: Indiana University Press.

Zieliński T. 1885. *Die Gliedering der altattischen Komödie*. Leipzig: Teubner.

Index